Learning to Read the Numbers

Being a critical reader of numerical information is an integral part of being literate in today's data-drenched world. Uniquely addressing both mathematics and language issues, this text shows how critical readers dig beneath the surface of data to better evaluate their usefulness and to understand how numbers are constructed by authors to portray a certain version of reality. Engaging, concise, and rich with examples and clear connections to classroom practice, it provides a framework of critical questions that children and teachers can pose to crack open authors' intentions, expose their decisions, and make clear who are the winners and losers—questions that are essential for building democratic classrooms.

Explaining and illustrating how K-8 teachers can engage students in developing the ability to be both critical composers and critical readers of texts, *Learning to Read the Numbers* is designed for teacher education courses across the areas of language arts, mathematics, and curriculum studies, and for elementary teachers, administrators, and literacy and mathematics coaches.

David J. Whitin teaches mathematics education courses in the Elementary Education Department at Wayne State University.

Phyllis E. Whitin teaches language arts education courses in the Elementary Education Department at Wayne State University.

Learning to Read the Numbers
Integrating Critical Literacy and Critical Numeracy in K-8 Classrooms

David J. Whitin and Phyllis E. Whitin

A Co-publication of Routledge and the National Council of Teachers of English

Routledge
Taylor & Francis Group
NEW YORK AND LONDON

Routledge
711 Third Avenue,
New York, NY 10017, USA

National Council of
Teachers of English

National Council of Teachers of English
1111 W. Kenyon Road
Urbana, IL 61801–1096

First published 2011
by Routledge
711 Third Avenue, New York, NY 10017, USA

Simultaneously published in the UK
by Routledge
2 Park Square, Milton Park, Abingdon, Oxon OX14 4RN

Routledge is an imprint of the Taylor & Francis Group, an informa business

National Council of Teachers of English
1111 W. Kenyon Road
Urbana, IL 61801–1096
NCTE Stock Number: 27835

Typeset in Minion by
RefineCatch Limited, Bungay, Suffolk

Library of Congress Cataloging-in-Publication Data
Whitin, David Jackman, 1947–
  Learning to read the numbers : integrating critical literacy and critical
  numeracy in K-8 classrooms / David J. Whitin and Phyllis Whitin.
    p. cm.
  "A Co-publication of Routledge and the National Council of Teachers of
  English."
  Includes bibliographical references and index.
  1. Language arts (Elementary).   2. Language arts—Correlation with
  content subjects.   3. Mathematics—Study and teaching (Elementary).
  I. Whitin, Phyllis.   II. National Council of Teachers of English.
  III. Title.
  LB1576W486282 2010
  372.6—dc22   2010013447

ISBN 13: 978–0–415–87430–4 (hbk)
ISBN 13: 978–0–415–87431–1 (pbk)
ISBN 13: 978–0–203–84266–9 (ebk)

Contents

Preface

It is our conviction that the integration of language and mathematics has profound implications for fostering a critical perspective in our schools. In this book we show that when numbers are embedded in an argument or used as a policy justification, people are often reluctant to question them. We surmise that this genuflecting before numerical information is due to people's learned trust in numbers. "Who am I to question the 'facts?' " some might ask.

To counter this prevailing attitude, we argue that mathematical information is a human construct, and not a sacrosanct edifice of unassailable truths. Just like language, data should be interrogated. Yet numbers have this abstract, scientific, apolitical aura that often makes them impervious to challenge and debate. This perception about the nature of mathematics has concerned us for some time. In our book we endeavor to make this problem explicit and to show that children, even young ones, can begin to understand that since numbers are constructed they can also be questioned, challenged. and revised.

In Chapter 1 we outline the pervasiveness of statistical texts in our world and advocate the cultivation of critics who analyze and evaluate these texts. We support this argument by citing researchers in the field of language and mathematics who urge the development of this critical thinking. We introduce a model and a heuristic that describe different aspects of the data-gathering process and that offer a critical frame for interrogating data-infused texts.

In Chapter 2 we examine in more depth how the wording and format of a question in a survey can affect the results. We discuss the complexities within seemingly "simple" questions, and show how motives, ideology, and other social factors are embedded in the questions one poses.

The issue of the definition of terms and the categorization of the data are the focus of Chapter 3. We argue that how one defines a term, such as homelessness or unemployment, determines what gets counted, and it is through these definitions that authors of texts construct their version of reality that positions others to view the world in particular ways. Decisions that authors also make about which categories to use, omit, or combine play a significant role in concealing some relationships and revealing others.

In Chapter 4 we show that visual texts, just like any form of communication, are not neutral but reflect an author's interests, values, and beliefs. Since there is no one-to-one correspondence between a set of data and its visual referent, authors have choices about how to represent those data. Their decisions about the visual display of the data can clarify some ideas and obfuscate others.

We illustrate the power of this decision-making by exploring how alternative ways to display the same data can tell quite different stories.

In Chapter 5 we highlight how any report of statistical information is only a partial account. When choices are made about data some information is always sacrificed. We discuss limitations, such as the nature of the sample, the relationship between results and conclusions, and the potential benefits and drawbacks to certain mathematical choices. Some of these mathematical choices include deciding whether to use absolute or relative (ratio) data; or to express average through the mean, median or mode. Each choice can frame an issue or problem from a different perspective.

Finally, in Chapter 6 we show how the integration of critical literacy and critical numeracy develops over time as a group of fifth-grade students gathered data about television advertisements directed at children. They researched marketing strategies, gathered data about cereals, and constructed survey instruments for their peers. They used their analysis of those data to create an informational PowerPoint presentation for their classmates and to write letters of protest to politicians and governmental and corporate agencies.

Throughout the book we present examples of children's work as well as examples from the media. In this way we show how the same critical issues permeate the construction of all texts. Children are doing the real work of any author as they grapple with the same problems, negotiate the same tensions, and confront the same limitations. Ideology and motives are always embedded in the work. The personal interests and intentions that even young children have about their social worlds are mirrored in the same way by companies and governmental agencies.

Another important idea threaded throughout this book is that children must be both critical composers as well as critical readers of texts. We argue that this ability begins with teachers giving children regular opportunities to create their own data-infused texts. As children confront the challenges of posing questions, defining terms, categorizing the data, and creating a visual representation, they come to understand the complexities of the task. They also come to realize that all these choices they have affect the results they receive, and this choosing is a form of power and control. Only as they experience these insights as authors themselves can they use this perspective to critique the statistical claims of others.

We wrote this book for classroom teachers K-8 as well as university instructors who teach classes in curricular issues, critical literacy, as well as the content areas of mathematics, English language arts, social studies, and science. We intend the book for several audiences because we view this critical stance as a perspective that cuts across all grades and all areas of the curriculum. It is work that every educator must be involved in if we are to create the kind of democratic schooling that the twenty-first century demands.

Acknowledgments

We are grateful to the many teachers and children with whom we have worked over the years, most recently the fifth-grade students and their teachers who worked with us on the cafeteria and consumer projects. They were the ones who lit the way by showing us what was possible. We are grateful to Rheta Rubenstein, who provided energy, optimism, and a wealth of ideas and resources. We also wish to thank the readers whose perspectives helped us craft this book. Diane Parker served as a reader for several of our drafts and each time provided invaluable insights for the book's development. Our colleagues Poonam Arya and Craig Roney helped us to reshape and fine tune chapters, and Donna Carroll cheerfully shared her graphic design expertise in editing and formatting the images for this book. We extend a special thank you to our editor, Naomi Silverman, whose guidance, support, and good humor made the task a most enjoyable one.

1
Learning to Read the Numbers
It's Everybody's Business

> An innumerate citizen today is as vulnerable as the illiterate peasant of Gutenberg's time.
>
> Lynn Steen (Steen, 1997a, p. xxvii)

Let us start with a few short stories about data. A teacher recently told us an anecdote about her daughter. Her 9-year-old really wanted a cell phone for Christmas but her mother refused to consider the request. In order to bolster her argument her daughter decided to poll friends and family members to see what their opinions were about this issue of cell phone ownership. After reviewing her results she decided not to count the votes of anyone over 30 because "they are really too old to understand what a 9-year-old needs." She then added, "And besides, they are messing up my questionnaire!"

Here's a story from a different context: an undergraduate class in statistics in which our son was a student. The professor talked about his work as a consultant for businesses. He related, "The first question that I ask a company is, 'What is it that you want me to show?' I tell them that I can use whatever data they have to tell the story they want their customers, stockholders, or employees to hear."

Now take a minute and consider what these two stories have in common. What parallels do you see between this 9-year-old and a college professor? We're struck by the fact that both of these individuals see data as a potential for power. They know that data can be used to persuade. They both also realize that data can be manipulated to support their own personal agendas. Similarly, they understand that a given set of data does not tell the whole story. They both recognized their power to decide what data to reveal and what to conceal.

If we look beneath the surface of these stories, we can infer several assumptions about what it means to be fully literate in today's information age:

- Data-related texts, like all communication, are not value-free (Gee, 1992, 1996; Huff, 1954; Janks, 2010; Luke & Freebody, 1999).
- Especially due to mass media and the internet, people encounter data-related texts with increasing frequency and in wider contexts (Best, 2001; Steen, 2001a, 2001b).
- Data-related texts are multimodal; they incorporate language, as well as visual and numerical information (Jewitt & Kress, 2003; Steen, 2007a; Tufte, 1983).

1

- Interpreting data-related texts involves exposing the choices that were made in the creation of these texts (Best, 2008; Spirer, Spirer & Jaffe, 1998; Whitin, P. & Whitin, D. J., 2008).

These insights about twenty-first century literacies cut across all subject fields. A critical orientation toward statistics supports learners to exercise their essential democratic responsibilities as they participate in a range of personal, social, and civic contexts (Cope & Kalantzis, 2000). This critical stance is a call to examine how people use these tools of mathematics, language, and visual representation in the fields of science and the social sciences. From this perspective the development of a critic's perspective is everybody's business (Steen, 1999, 2007b).

This book primarily involves the fields of mathematics and language but also shows how children use these tools in a variety of contexts, including social studies and science. In the remaining sections of this chapter we will look at what scholars in both fields have been saying about being a critical reader. We will then describe a conceptual model and heuristic we have developed to integrate these perspectives. Finally, we share some classroom examples to illustrate how the questions in the heuristic may be used as an instructional guide.

Theoretical Perspectives from Mathematics

We live in an age that is inundated with data. Look around and see where you encounter data in your daily rounds. Perhaps you'll find data in the pharmacy where you notice on a tube of antibacterial cream that it is recommended as the #1 cream by dermatologists. Or perhaps you will see data at the grocery store where "mom preferred" is advertised on the front of a child's cereal box. When you look on the internet you might see a new diet formula which claims that 93% of women who were on this diet lost on average five pounds per week. Or perhaps when you turn on the television you hear a politician claiming that the economy is in good shape because the number of available jobs is increasing. In each case, data (or the implied use of data) are used to persuade. Marketers, politicians, and anyone else with an agenda to promote know that their chances of convincing the public about a certain product or issue are greatly enhanced if they can attach a number to their argument. They know that most people don't question numbers. Most people don't think about the way that issues of motives, power, and ideology come into play when numbers are used for social purposes (Borasi, 1989; Gee, 1992). There are colloquial expressions which people often use that convey this widespread belief in the inherent truth in numbers: Numbers don't lie; the facts speak for themselves; the facts tell us . . . The verbs of "lie," "speak," and "tell" anthropomorphize the term "data" by bestowing on it human qualities. In this way the term "data" takes on an agency unto itself. The anthropomorphic language not only hides the identity of the authors of this numerical information but also makes the data seem more detached, abstract and therefore unlikely to be challenged.

So while the general public is often intimidated by numbers, the world continues to be awash with increasing amounts of numerical information. As Orrill (1997) notes, computers generate data "every time a purchase is made, a poll is taken, a disease is diagnosed, or a satellite passes over a section of terrain" (p. xvi). There is both a boon and a bane to this seemingly unlimited access to numerical information. The advantage is that now not only specialists, but everyone, can read the data about the latest nutritional studies, the risks of taking certain medications, and so forth. "Potentially, if put to good use, this unprecedented access to numerical information promises to place more power in the hands of individuals and serve as a stimulus to democratic discourse and civic decision making" (Orrill, 1997, p. xvi). However, there are also dangers in such a data-driven society. If individuals are not able to think critically about these data, then they cannot participate in meaningful discussions about what these numbers mean. In light of such dangers Lynn Steen has issued this dire warning: "In short, an innumerate citizen today is as vulnerable as the illiterate peasant of Gutenberg's time" (Steen, 1997a, p. xxvii). This state of affairs has profound implications for educators.

Robert Moses, in his compelling account of the Algebra Project in *Radical equations* (Moses & Cobb, 2001), points out that this issue of mathematical illiteracy is particularly pronounced for underserved populations. He calls mathematical literacy the new "civil right," and its development is as urgent an issue "as the lack of registered Black voters in Mississippi was in 1961" (p. 5). He extends this parallel further by arguing that mathematical literacy is particularly pervasive with Blacks and other minorities, "making them the designated serfs of the information age" (p. 11). Thus, the struggle for mathematical (and science) literacy is a struggle for citizenship, equality, and freedom (p. 14). Moses recognizes the demands of the data-drenched age in which we live and calls for citizens who are competent in evaluating and interpreting those numbers.

Nurturing a critical perspective in mathematics is supported by two important instructional emphases: (1) teaching for understanding; and (2) connecting mathematics across the disciplines. Being a critic of statistical texts requires an understanding of the mathematics as well as an understanding of how people create and use numerical information in various contexts. Since the publication of its *Principles and standards for school mathematics* (2000), the National Council of Teachers of Mathematics has taken a leading role in promoting teaching for understanding. Some of its standards include communication, representation, connections, and reasoning and proof. It is a call for a curriculum that encourages questioning, argumentation, and problem posing, as well as multiple forms of representation, such as writing, drawing, graphical displays, and models. These efforts by NCTM are intended to combat a transmission model of teaching and learning that has dominated mathematics teaching in the past, and is still a persistent voice in the "math wars" discussions of today. Jo Boaler succinctly described this transmission model as: Learning without thought, Learning without talking, Learning without reality (2008). Alan Bishop has labeled such teaching as "a technique-oriented curriculum" that emphasizes mathematics as a way of doing rather than as a way of knowing (1991, p. 3). This kind of curriculum "cannot help understanding, cannot develop meaning, cannot enable the learner to develop a critical stance either inside or outside mathematics" (p. 8). It shuts off any personal interpretation, invention and opinion (p. 9). Bishop argues that what is needed is a recognition that education—and by extension, mathematics education—is a social process. And yet, "the social, the human, the essentially interpersonal nature of education is so often ignored in the rush for the acquisition of mathematical techniques and in the desire for so-called efficiency in mathematics education" (pp. 13–14).

Recognition of mathematics as a social process reinforces the belief that it is a human-construct, and may therefore be examined and critiqued. Thus, connecting mathematics to other subject fields means viewing it in its sociopolitical contexts. This aspect of mathematical learning has been largely side-stepped by NCTM (Apple, 1992; Williams & Joseph, 1993). However, if students are to be the kinds of critics who are essential to the civic discourse of a democracy, they must come to understand how people use numbers to wield power, promote arguments, and influence public policy. Bishop states, "At the societal level mathematics is mediated by various institutions in society and is subject to the political and ideological forces in that society" (p. 14). Mathematics and science are not ethically and morally neutral enterprises but have an increased social responsibility to explore its uses in their social and political contexts (Ernest, 1989). Unless these contexts become a regular part of the learning of mathematics the social significance of mathematics is lost, and mathematics becomes a field of abstract calculations rather than meaningful interpretations. Ernest (1989, p. 202) issues this sharp warning to the mathematics field:

> Can we hide behind the argument that we only provide the metaphor and concepts for the dehumanization of social issues and that therefore our hands are clean? If providing such tools leaves the tool-maker free from responsibility, is not the same true for weapon manufacturers?

When the National Council of Teachers of Mathematics published its first *Curriculum and evaluation standards for school mathematics* in 1989 Michael Apple rebuked them for not addressing this socio-political dimension. He claims that one of the major responsibilities of educators is to support our students "to critically assess the nature of truth claims, and the uses and abuses of knowledge they are being asked to learn" (Apple 1992, p. 423). He continues his argument by asserting that the high status granted to mathematical knowledge in the various reform efforts has nothing to do with its elegant formulas, internal beauty, or its conceptual ways of knowing the world, "but because of its socioeconomic utility for those who already possess economic capital" (p. 423). Even though the Standards were revised in 2000 we believe that Apple's criticisms are still appropriate and justified. Thus, a critical perspective in mathematics cannot be developed unless students have regular opportunities to use it for real purposes. In this way they can recognize the role of context in their work, and examine the choices and decisions they make as a set of a much larger pool of possibilities. A critical perspective also entails a close examination of mathematical concepts. Such concepts as time, ratio, area, and average may be known as generalizations in the narrow confines of a textbook. But out in the real world they become tools that authors use to frame an issue or build an argument. It is this critical interrogation of concepts *in use* that the mathematics field has largely ignored.

Perspectives from Literacy Theory

The attention that English language arts educators pay to the critical dimensions of literacy can offer perspectives and strategies for developing a similar orientation toward statistics. Although this discipline has its own history of struggles against a transmission model of teaching, the field has historically taken a persistent stand about the relationship between literacy and civic responsibility. Participants at the 2005 Conference on English Education Leadership and Policy Summit articulate this stance: "English education, more than any other academic discipline, because of its focus on language and representation, contributes vitally to the processes by which society defines, understands, maintains, and *transforms* itself" (Alsup et. al., 2006, p. 279, emphasis in original).

In recent years scholars in the field of literacy have been stressing the relationships among developing technologies, societal changes, and the critical dimension of reading and composing. The definition of what it means to be literate is an evolving one, and thus incorporates new dimensions in the twenty-first century (Leu, Kinzer, Coiro, & Cammack, 2004; National Council of Teachers of English, 2008). We're arguing here that the increasing production and availability of statistical texts makes it imperative to embrace numeracy as an essential part of these literacies. Theoretical perspectives about reading and composing and their instructional implications apply to mathematical contexts.

We see Luke and Freebody's four resource model (1999) as a means for understanding and acting upon numeracy within a critical literacy framework. It is rooted in sociocultural theory that defines texts as expressive forms infused with a particular social group's ways of thinking, valuing, and believing (Fairclough, 2000; Gee, 1992, 1996; Janks, 2010). The model names four interdependent sets of practices that describe effective reading and composing. As we will illustrate below, these practices involve the reader-composer as *code breaker* (graphophonemics), *meaning maker* (semantics), *text user* (pragmatics), and *text critic*. Although these four practices are identified separately for the purpose of explaining them, in actual communication they work together.

Let us examine how these four practices apply to readers of language as well as of statistical texts. For convenience, we will consider the model from the perspective of reading. As a *code-breaker*, a reader of a language-based text must understand print concepts, such as the alphabetic principle (symbols on the page represent sounds of speech) and structural patterns (ways in which symbols are visually organized on the page). Similarly, readers of statistical texts must also understand mathematical concepts such as ratio, and structural conventions such as x and y axes. As *meaning makers*, readers in both contexts use their experiential and cultural knowledge to make sense of texts. For example, children who have recently visited the city zoo can draw upon that experience as they read books or interpret graphs and charts about animals in the rain forest. As *text users*, learners gain knowledge about different forms and genres by reading and composing texts for many purposes. For literary texts, readers learn through experience that reading poetry involves a different style of reading from reading a persuasive essay, while readers of statistical texts adjust in parallel ways as they interpret line graphs versus bar charts.

In Luke and Freebody's words, being a *text critic* involves "acting on the knowledge that texts are not ideologically natural or neutral" (1999, sec. 3, ¶3). Text critics dig beneath the surface to uncover implicit messages. They ask questions about power, whose knowledge is privileged, or whose voice is absent or marginalized in a given text. In a literary example, a *text critic* reading a historical account might note whose point of view is portrayed, as well as whose is not. A *text critic* of a data-related text might raise questions about who was and who was not included in the sampled population, or who is privileged or silenced by visually representing data in aggregated or disaggregated form. Luke and Freebody's notion of critical competence therefore encompasses the interrogation of the language, visual, and numerical aspects of data-related texts.

Instructionally, Luke and Freebody's model advocates that children need experience with all four aspects beginning in the early grades and throughout their formal education (1999). The four resources complement each another; they do not progress in a sequential fashion with a critical perspective saved for last. For instance, readers cannot be critics without having knowledge about a range of text forms or genres. Conversely, they are not fully competent text users or meaning makers unless they understand that the text forms themselves are permeated by messages of status, power, and ideology.

Even when working with young children, teachers can encourage them to express multiple points of view by raising such questions as: Whose voice do we not hear in the story? What do you think they would say? (Vasquez, 2010). Likewise, teachers in the mathematics classroom also have a parallel responsibility. Later in this chapter we will describe a heuristic designed to develop the habit of mind of "second-guessing texts" (Luke & Freebody, 1999, sec. 2, 10) that incorporate data. This disposition involves probing beneath the surface to uncover the assumptions, expose motives, and raise issues about power and control. Like critical literary prompts, portions of the heuristic may be used even with very young children (Whitin, 2006; Whitin, P. & Whitin, D. J., 2008).

It is important to stress that this critical orientation applies to both reading and writing. This dual application relates to another valuable perspective from literacy theory. Literacy educators have long recognized the connections between these two processes. When children have the opportunity to write regularly and for a range of purposes, they bring their knowledge of the composing process to the reading process (National Council of Teachers of English, 2004; Portalupi & Fletcher, 2001). From a critical literacy perspective, they can understand how texts reflect the values and personal, social, and cultural experiences of the author (Vasquez, 2010). Children with this insider's knowledge of authoring are well equipped to raise critical questions about the texts they read. From a mathematical perspective, children should regularly collect and represent data, particularly data that relate to their personal interests, experiences, and knowledge (Curcio, 2001; Schwartz & Whitin, 2006; Williams & Joseph, 1993). They need opportunities to discuss, examine, and interpret their work with their teachers and peers. Through these experiences they can become proficient in creating and communicating texts, as well as in critiquing texts made by others. Moreover, the process is recursive; experience with critiquing texts as readers fuels more informed composing.

Finally, perspectives about multimodal communication also contribute to the quest for developing a critical orientation toward data. Although all texts are multimodal (i.e., there are visual elements such as font and spatial arrangement in print texts), the rise of digital technologies has expanded ways in which verbal, visual, audio, and animation elements may be combined to express ideas (Jewitt & Kress, 2003; Kress, 2000; National Council of Teachers of English, 2004). This trend has led to increased attention to the potentials of nonlinguistic modes, particularly visual forms, to express ideas and relationships. Of course, expressive forms other than language incorporate ideological factors as well. In the case of statistical texts, a graph visually represents quantified data and guides the reader to make comparisons. At the same time, its abstract quality can convey a sense of authority and objectivity that distances the reader from the social context behind the text (Gee, 1992; Kress, 2000, 2003). These tenets of multimodal theory offer educators additional ways to understand the unquestioned trust that many people have developed toward numerical information. Thus, from a multiliteracies perspective a critical stance toward data involves interrogating all modes of expression represented in a text. In statistical texts, word choice and definitions of terms matter. The design of visual display matters. The ways data are collected and categorized matter. Since statistical texts are multimodal, reading and composing data-related texts is an interdisciplinary venture. It's everyone's business.

A Conceptual Model and Heuristic for Critiquing the Data

We developed the conceptual model and heuristic (Figures 1.1 and 1.2) as a guide for promoting this critical perspective. In the model, "Social Context" is the all-encompassing band that emphasizes how statistical texts are products of social activity, and are therefore infused with cultural values, power relations, and personal agendas (Borasi, 1992; Gee, 1992, 1996; Borasi & Segal, 2001). Dimensions of statistical texts noted in the inner ring are based on the work of Darrell Huff, whose classic book, *How to lie with statistics* (1954), shows how these texts are constructed to represent a particular point of view. The critic's perspective occupies the central core. The double-pointed arrows emanating from this core show that a critic interrogates statistical texts as both a reader and composer. As children are given regular opportunities to compose their own statistical texts, the more they gain an insider's knowledge about how

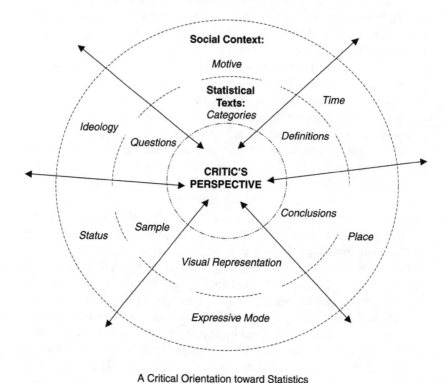

A Critical Orientation toward Statistics

Figure 1.1 Conceptual Model of a Critical Orientation toward Statistics.

these texts are constructed. Their knowledge about the process gives them valuable insights for interrogating the texts of others.

The heuristic in Figure 1.2 elaborates upon this critic's perspective by encouraging children to interrogate results, challenge assumptions, and uncover biases. These questions also support critics to consider the choices that people have made about what to count, how to count, and what the data mean (Best, 2001, 2008). In this process of raising questions and imagining alternatives children learn that choices are just a set of a larger pool of possibilities. And it is the element of choice that reflects bias.

We will now turn to some examples of statistical texts to demonstrate the heuristic (Figure 1.2) in action. Aspects of the Social Context (#1), particularly "the motive," can be illustrated by an example from the news media (Burros, 2007, p. A15). It was reported that research studies financed by the food industry, as well as studies by pharmaceutical companies, were much more likely to produce favorable results about company products compared to research that was independently financed. Companies obviously have a vested interest in producing studies that show favorable (or at least neutral) results. In one examination of nutrition studies the authors found that of the 24 studies of soft drinks, milk, and juice that were financed by the industry, 21 had results favorable or neutral to the industry, and three were unfavorable. Of the 52 studies that were *not* financed by the industry, 32 were favorable or neutral and 20 were unfavorable. This discrepancy in results raises questions about the motives of the food industry. It underscores the importance of skeptical citizens who need to pose such questions as, "Who financed this study?"; "What were their reasons for conducting this study?"; "What were they hoping to find out?" In this way motives become more transparent for all to consider.

Another aspect of Figure 1.2 is "The Question," (#2) which examines how the wording of a question can affect the results. An example comes from the debate over gun control. Advocates for gun control have posed this survey question to bolster their position: "Do you favor cracking down on illegal gun sales?" Since most people favor stopping illegal activity, gun-control activists have effectively used these data in their argument. However, the National Rifle Association has posed a different question designed to support their point of view: "Would you favor or oppose a law giving police the power to decide who may or may not own a firearm?" As expected, most respondents opposed giving the police such broad power, and the NRA then argued that most Americans oppose gun control (Best, 2001, p. 48). Critics know to ask questions about the question. In this way they better understand how a given set of results was obtained.

Next, the heuristic includes "The Definitions" (#3) and "The Categories" (#4). For instance, attempts to categorize the ethnicity of the American population means that some of the richness of that diversity is lost. Classifying a

Questions to Support a Critical Orientation toward Statistics

Features	Critic's Perspective	Questions to Consider
1. The Social Context	The researcher's motives, the setting, and the status of participants influence all aspects of the process.	What is your purpose for collecting this information? Who is your audience? How are you collecting this information?
2. The Question	The way a question is posed influences the kinds of responses one receives.	How did you ask your question? Why did you ask it in that way? How might this language have influenced the responses you received? What groups of people did your question privilege? Silence? How else might the question have been worded?
3. The Definitions	Broad or narrow definitions determine what gets counted. The choice of words reflects the intentions of the author.	How did you define this word? Why did you define it this way rather than another way? What groups of people did your definition or choice of words privilege? Silence?
4. The Categories	Data can be aggregated or disaggregated to serve one's purposes.	How were the categories decided upon? What happened to responses that did not fit into these categories? In what other ways might you categorize these data? What information is lost by using these categories?
5. The Visual Representation	Displays can reveal and conceal certain layers of information.	Why did you decide to show your information in this way? What information is concealed/ revealed by this form of representation? Who benefits from representing the data in this way? How else could you have displayed your data?
6. The Sample	The knowledge, background, interests and biases of the sampled population influence their responses.	Who did you ask? How informed was the sampled population about this topic? What might have happened if you had asked a different group of people?
7. The Conclusions	Conclusions are based upon the assumptions of the researchers.	How are your results different from your conclusions? What conclusions can't we make? How might your choice of a mathematical concept (ratio, average) influence your audience's thinking?

Figure 1.2 Heuristic for A Critic's Orientation toward Statistics. Adapted from *Thinking and reasoning with data and chance: sixty-eighth yearbook*, copyright 2006 by the National Council of Teachers of Mathematics.

segment of the population as Asian hides the specific number of Japanese, Chinese, Laotian, and so on. A similar problem exists with definitions. How do state and national governments know how many homeless people there are? (Jackson & Jamieson, 2007). It depends on one's definition. Is it only those who show up at designated shelters? If so, how long do they have to stay to be counted? One night? One month? What about people who live out on the streets, under bridges, in city parks? What about people who live with friends or relatives because they cannot afford a place of their own? In short, critics know to ask questions about how terms are defined because definitions can expand or narrow what gets counted. And important public policy decisions are made based on what people choose to count.

The process of "Visual Representation" is addressed in #5. How people choose to display data can reveal and/or conceal certain relationships. For instance, children might track the highest daily temperature for one month and represent these data on a line graph (see Figure 1.3 as an example). However, they could use these same data on a bar graph by grouping together days in the 40s, 50s, 60s, and so on (Figure 1.4). This bar graph does not show the daily fluctuations in temperature that occurred over this time period. Conversely, it might be easier to compare ranges of temperature on the bar graph. Each form of representation illuminates certain relationships and hides others.

"The Sample" (#6) and "The Conclusions" (#7) are the remaining two dimensions of this data-gathering process found in Figure 1.2. The sample used can limit the conclusions one can claim. For instance, suppose a health magazine conducted a survey of its readers and found that 75% of the respondents exercise regularly each week. What if the magazine then claimed that most Americans are really health-conscious and are being blamed unfairly by the media and health experts for their supposed lack of physical activity? Critics might question whether this sample of subscribers to a health magazine was truly representative of the general population. They might also challenge the difference between the *results* and *conclusions.* Although the *results* supposedly show that 75% do claim to exercise, it would be unfair to *conclude* that this percentage represents the entire population.

One way that teachers might promote this critical orientation toward statistics is to pose the kinds of questions described in Figure 1.2. The following two classroom examples highlight many of the dimensions of this heuristic. In the first example the teachers' questions support fifth-grade children to confront the inherent biases of data collection and representation. In the second example kindergarten children's observations of a graph led to a discussion about the incomplete nature of the data representation. Both examples demonstrate that children of any age can develop a critical stance if the data are connected to a familiar context.

Fifth Graders Learn to Critique their own Data

From time to time throughout this book we will be sharing some collaborative work we did with fifth-grade students and their teachers over a two-year period. We were interested in promoting a critical stance toward data in the context of their mathematics and language curricular goals. As we examined the grade-level expectations for fifth grade we identified several objectives in both of these areas. For instance, the children needed to understand the various uses

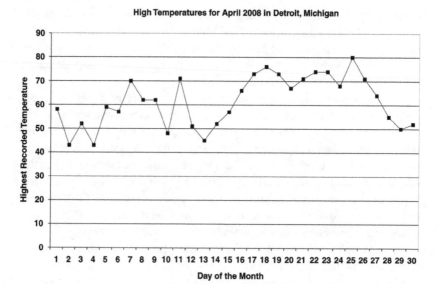

Figure 1.3 and 1.4 A line graph (1.3) and a bar graph (1.4) convey different kinds of information about the same data.

of the bar, line, and pie charts in mathematics. In language arts they needed to analyze how authors used graphs to summarize ideas and promote a particular point of view for various audiences. The story we tell here focuses on the work of two children who were involved in our first data-gathering experience. This opening story helps to show how teachers can begin to promote a critical stance toward data with children who were inexperienced with critical analysis, especially in mathematics. The children surveyed their classmates, recorded the results, and shared their findings with their peers. During this process we looked for opportunities to pose questions to highlight various critical dimensions of the data-gathering process that are outlined in the heuristic (Figure 1.2). Some of these dimensions that the girls encountered included: the social context (#1), the wording of the question (#2), definitions (#3), the categories (#4), the visual representation (#5), the information not conveyed (#7), and the potential effect of different sampled populations (#6).

After brainstorming a few possible survey ideas, Nakia and Desirée decided on the topic of family chores. They agreed to pose the following question to their peers: "What is your least favorite chore and why?" The structure and language of this question, as well as the social context, later became a focus for critique. As the girls interviewed their peers, Phyllis noticed that several respondents hesitated to answer this question. Afterwards, she brought this observation to the children's attention. She remarked, "I noticed that some students didn't answer right away. I wonder what they were thinking?" The girls recalled especially how one boy paused for several seconds, and Desirée exclaimed, "Maybe he was just making something up!" They further noted that other children had not answered the question as it was posed. One girl had answered, "Nothing. I want to keep the house clean," and another had replied, "Nothing. I don't do chores." Based on these responses, Desirée and Nakia began to wonder if some classmates did not have a least favorite chore, but felt compelled to answer the question the way it was worded (#2). How valid were their findings? Perhaps some people may have been silenced by the way their question was posed (#1, #2). These initial misgivings showed the emergence of a critical stance toward their data.

Phyllis raised another language-related issue: the definition of "chore" (#3). She remarked, "I noticed that some people said, 'What?' when you asked the question, and one child answered, 'Making my bed.' Is that a chore or just a routine? What about bringing your dishes to the sink when you finish a meal? Would that count as a 'chore?'" Nakia replied, "Some things like that you just do out of respect for your family." Now the children wondered if the word, "jobs," would have been a better way to distinguish between "chore" and "routine". Part of a teacher's role is to invite children to closely examine their language and to entertain alternative interpretations of that language. In this case, it is quite possible that these children had varying definitions for "chore." Thus, the language we choose to use can affect the data we receive.

In light of these concerns about the language used, how might the girls proceed? Phyllis suggested, "Do you think we should ask the class about how they felt about the question?" They agreed. When the girls shared their findings with the class later they asked their peers if some had really had no "least favorite chore." Half a dozen children raised their hands. The girls also told the class that when they tabulated the data they realized they did not know people's reasons for doing chores. Some people might do chores to help their families. On the other hand, some parents might assign chores as a form of punishment. Several children in the class nodded in agreement with this last suggestion. This part of the discussion highlighted that there were limits to what their data revealed (#7). It also showed that there was a difference between results and conclusions (#7). The results show 20 people had *named* a least favorite chore but one cannot conclude that all of them truly *had* a least favorite chore.

Phyllis also raised the issue with the entire class concerning the sampled population (#6). Would the results have been different if second graders or eighth graders had been polled? The children felt the data would definitely have been different. Various children suggested that second graders might not have many chores to discuss, and they might enjoy chores more because they would feel grown up. In contrast, the eighth graders "might have more chores they didn't like" (e.g., mowing the lawn). This brief discussion highlighted for the children that the data one receives can be influenced by the population that one chooses to sample.

When the children constructed their first graph, "Least Favorite Chore," additional issues arose (#5). They began by making a rough draft on the whiteboard. They drew an x and y axis and labeled the y with multiples of 5, i.e., 5, 10, 15, 20, 25 (Figure 1.5). Next they made bars to represent the totals for their categories: 1, 5, and 6. Of course, given this scale, the bars looked almost the same size. Phyllis pointed out this problem of representation and suggested that the girls consider making a different scale. Nakia suggested counting by 1s so that the differences among the height of the bars would be more accentuated

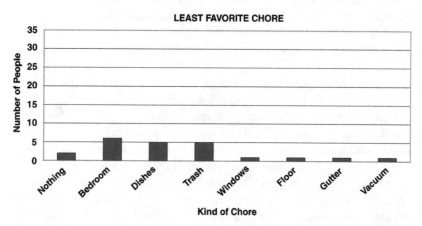

Figure 1.5 First draft of "Least Favorite Chore" graph (Copied from whiteboard).

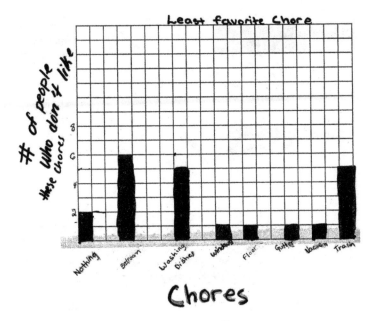

Figure 1.6 Revised graph of "Least Favorite Chore".

Source: Whitin, P. & Whitin, D. J. (2008). Learning to read the numbers: A critical orientation toward statistics. *Language Arts*, 85 (6), 432–441. Copyright 2008 by the National Council of Teachers of English. Used with permission.

(Figure 1.6). In retrospect, we realized we could have further deepened the girls' understanding by having them analyze the effect of using several different scales. Just as they saw how a scale of 5s could minimize the differences, we could have challenged them to see how decreasing the scale, such as a scale of ¼, could maximize these differences. (Of course, proportionately, the differences between categories remain constant despite the scale.) From a critical perspective, we saw that this aspect of their work had been a missed opportunity for exploring how people might use different scales to influence what the viewer concludes (Huff, 1954).

The girls faced another dilemma as they made categories (#4) for their second graph, "Reasons Not to Like Chores" (Figure 1.7). They had recorded each person's unique reason for why the chore was their least favorite (Figure 1.8). The girls were a little hesitant on how next to proceed because the reasons seemed so different from each other. Phyllis suggested that they look for similarities in the responses in order to make categories. They initially identified a category of "Took too long" with such statements as, "I have a lot of stuff to do," and "It takes a long time." They created another category entitled "Boring" with such statements as, "I don't want to do it," and "I don't like doing it." Then they decided to collapse these two categories into one called,

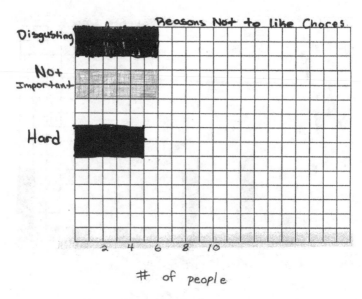

Figure 1.7 Graph of "Reasons Not to Like Chores".

"Not important," because they reasoned, "If you really thought it was important it wouldn't be boring!"

They created another category called "Disgusting." This included such comments as, "Taking out the trash because it gets my hands dirty" or "Doing dishes because my little brother leaves nasty things on his plate." However, there was one child who said that he didn't like doing dishes because "It feels like I am taking a bath." The girls decided to include this comment under "Disgusting" because they inferred that he didn't like taking baths and preferred showers. They admitted that they really couldn't be sure of his thinking. At this point, Desirée commented, "My teacher says that making a graph is easy. But it's not that easy if you're trying to make categories!" Since the children owned the process they were aware of the many complex decisions they had to make along the way. Thus, this initial graphing experience laid an important foundation for the girls to critique other data-related texts.

Phyllis wanted the girls to think further about the biased nature of their categories. She added, "Other people might not completely agree with your categories, like 'Not important' and 'Disgusting.' " Realizing the power that she and Nakia had as authors, Desirée replied, "We have more of the opinion. They [their classmates] don't have as much of the say. It's coming out the way *we're* saying it. We might see it as something different and maybe not what *they* were thinking." She clearly understood that as authors, the girls were the ones with the power to decide what the topic was, how the question was to be worded, and which categories were to be established (#1). In doing so they might be silencing some of the voices of their classmates (Vasquez, 2010). Recognizing

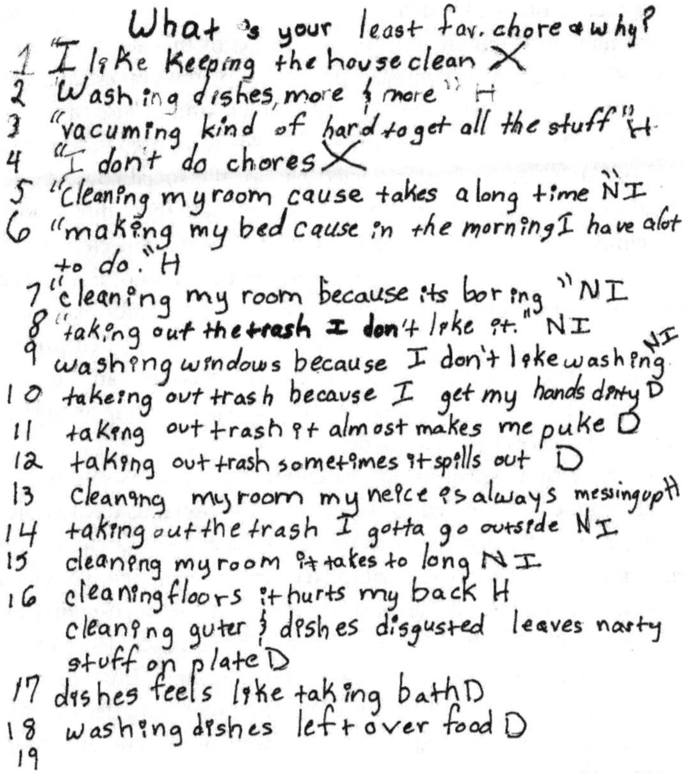

What 's your least fav. chore & why?
1 I like Keeping the house clean X
2 Washing dishes, more & more " H
3 "vacuming kind of hard to get all the stuff" H
4 "I don't do chores X
5 "Cleaning my room cause takes a long time NI
6 "making my bed cause in the morning I have alot
   to do." H
7 "cleaning my room because its boring " NI
8 "taking out the trash I don't like it." NI
9 washing windows because I don't like washing NI
10 takeing out trash because I get my hands dirty D
11 taking out trash it almost makes me puke D
12 taking out trash sometimes it spills out D
13 Cleaning my room my neice is always messing up H
14 taking out the trash I gotta go outside NI
15 cleaning my room it takes to long NI
16 cleaning floors it hurts my back H
   cleaning guter & dishes disgusted leaves nasty
   stuff on plate D
17 dishes feels like taking bathD
18 washing dishes left over food D
19

Figure 1.8 Survey data for the question, "What is Your Least Favorite Chore and Why?"
The responses have been marked with "H" ("hard"), NI ("not important"), "D" (disgusting), or "X" (no least favorite chore). "X" responses were not recorded on the graph.

this relationship of power helps to demonstrate that data are something that humans construct, and so they can be questioned, debated, and critiqued.

Kindergarten Children as Critics

Even simple and commonly used graphing investigations can become a context for developing a critical stance. In this next example, some kindergarten children created a graph of their favorite kinds of apples (Whitin, D. J. & Whitin, P., 2003). In contrast to the previous example, it was the children rather than the adults who exposed the limitations of the graph and thus opened up opportunities for taking a critic's perspective.

In this all-day kindergarten, the teacher assistant made weekly trips to the grocery store to buy snacks. This routine provided a real purpose for the children to collect data about their food preferences (e.g., to buy the kind of fruit that they favored). One afternoon the children sampled slices of Granny Smith, yellow Delicious, and red Delicious apples. After tasting all three, they chose a favorite to record on a tally sheet. This preliminary activity relates to three dimensions named on Figure 1.2. In the context of this activity, "Asking the question" (#2) included the physical properties of the apples. In essence we adults were asking, "Of these three varieties, which kind of *sliced* apples do you like?" Similarly, the three choices (categories, #4) were predetermined by the adults, whose status as teachers reflected part of the social context (#1). It is ironic that we adults did not recognize and appreciate these dimensions until after the children had interrogated the data that were collected. As we discovered later, some of the children had responses that did not fit these choices, and they chose not to participate. However, like the fifth-grade example, it was because the children had a personal investment in the data (their preferences) that they were able to expose these biases. These issues came to light the following day when the children created and discussed a simple pictograph that represented the choices they had made.

During center time, small groups of children took turns selecting die-cut paper apples that corresponded to the color of the previous day's choices and glued them on to a large piece of chart paper. Later that morning, all of the children gathered to discuss the completed graph: eight red, six green, and three yellow. David initiated the conversation with the open-ended prompt, "What do you notice?" The conversation that ensued included comparisons ("There's more red than green or yellow"), and counting ("My favorite color is the highest: 1, 2, 3, 4, 5, 6, 7, 8"). However, when one child decided to count the total of all three columns and found 17, we were puzzled because there were 22 children in the class.

Here was an opportunity for us to invite the children to challenge the data. Phyllis remarked, "I'm surprised that we only have 17." Accustomed to the daily lunch and attendance count, the children exclaimed, "Hey! We have 22 people in the class!" They quickly realized that the previous day's absentees accounted for two of the missing responses. Ethan then quietly admitted, "I didn't vote yesterday." "What made you decide not to vote?" Phyllis asked. She was surprised by his answer: "The apples were cut up," he replied. "I like mine whole."

Ethan's response exposed the bias inherent in the way the "question" was asked, in this case by providing only sliced apples as choices. The present data display was therefore limited; it concealed the fact that Ethan did in fact like apples (#5). Giving the children the responsibility for changing the representation would afford them an opportunity to examine this critical dimension of data. Because the die-cut apples did look whole, David asked, "What could we do to show that these apples were really cut?" When one child suggested marking them with a line for a "slice mark," the others agreed, and Ethan added a green unmarked paper apple to the appropriate column. Noah, who had also declined to participate, now volunteered to add his red "whole" apple to the graph. Finally, Samantha expressed a second challenge to the representation: "I don't like sliced apples either. My momma cuts my apples into little triangles and I like them that way." Again David replied, "And how could you show that way on the graph?" Samantha confidently selected a yellow paper apple, cut it into tiny pieces, and glued this representation of her unique choice on to the graph (Figure 1.9).

The revised graph therefore showed both the children's preferences for each apple as well as the methods of preparation. In reflecting on the experience, the children realized that their alternative representation was more inclusive and therefore fairer. Voices that had been silenced (those who did not like sliced apples) were now recognized and heard (Vasquez, 2004). The recognition of these silenced voices also helped show that missing information is a common occurrence in the data-gathering process.

Although experiences with simple pictographs regularly occur in early childhood classrooms, we believe that several conditions contributed to the shift toward a critical examination of data. First, the children were invested in the discussion because their personal experiences and preferences were reflected in the data. Second, the initial question posed to the class, "What do you notice?," encouraged a wide range of responses and gave the children the responsibility for the analysis. Third, we invited the children to solve the problems they encountered. For example, we asked the children to investigate the anomaly of 17 apples. In addition, when the children discovered the limitation of the first visual representation, we challenged them to invent a way to revise the graph so that it would reveal what had been concealed, i.e., apple preparation.

We were humbled by this experience. These young learners' refusal to participate in the initial data experience enabled us to recognize the physical aspect of "the question" (sliced apples). We realized that by limiting the range of preparation choices and not inviting their perspectives, we marginalized the children's voices. This experience also reminded us of the importance of listening closely to children, remaining open to the unexpected. Once the inequities of the first graph were exposed, the children effectively re-represented the data to reflect additional layers of information and thus make their voices heard. Indeed, even the youngest of children are capable of taking a critic's perspective on data.

Looking Back and Looking Ahead

In this chapter one of the ideas we have been emphasizing is that interpreting statistical information is an integral part of literacy. Informed citizens in a democracy must be vigilant critics of this statistical onslaught so that they can expose the limitations and biases of the data they encounter. Because of the pervasiveness of statistics, the responsibility of nurturing a critic's perspective toward these data lies with teachers of all subjects and all ages. In this chapter we introduced a conceptual model and a heuristic that highlights

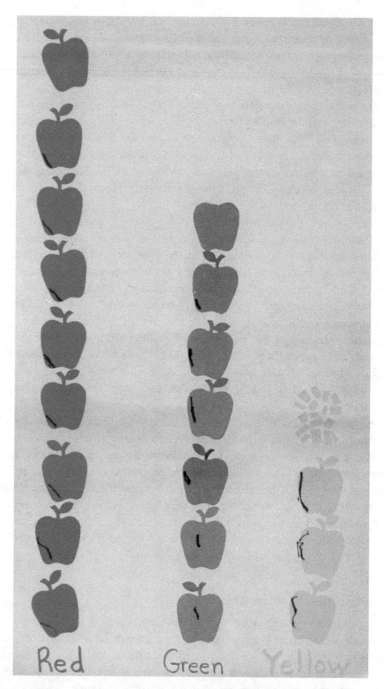

Figure 1.9 The revised apple graph. Reprinted with permission from *Teaching children mathematics*, copyright 2003 by the National Council of Teachers of Mathematics. All rights reserved.

some important guiding questions that readers can pose as they encounter statistical texts.

The stories from these kindergarten and fifth-grade children help show how this heuristic comes to life in the classroom. They also suggest some questions for further inquiry:

- Both graphs represented topics from the children's own knowledge and direct experience. The fifth graders chose their survey topic about chores based upon their conversations with friends. The kindergarten children brought their experiences with various ways to prepare apples to the class activity. *In what ways can teachers use children's knowledge, interests, and out-of-school experiences as contexts for data collection and representation? Are there issues on the playground, in the cafeteria, or in the classroom that could be addressed through data gathering, display, and analysis?*

- The children represented their data in different ways. The kindergarten children saw how their revisions to the original graph added new layers of information to the display. The fifth graders tried out two different scales for their graph. They could have pursued further how the manipulation of scales can dramatically change the representation of the same dataset. *What are contexts in which children might represent data in several ways and critique the results? In what ways can children construct and embed visual displays of data in their persuasive writing?*

- The fifth graders were challenged to consider how the phrasing of their question, "Least favorite chore" might have unfairly positioned people to respond in a particular way. *As authors, in what ways can children see how the language that they use affects the numbers they gather? What if they examined published graphs in magazines, newspapers and on the internet and discussed how certain questions were posed and how that language might have influenced the results?*

- The kindergarten children acted upon the limitations they found in the first graph and created a revised version. In this way they began to learn not to view a single set of data as the last word on an issue. *In what ways can graphing experiences be connected over time and across all content areas?*

- The fifth graders realized that they had the power to create the categories as they saw fit, even though some of their classmates might disagree. *In what ways can teachers help children to analyze what they choose to do or not to do as they gather and represent data?*

2

Getting What You Ask For

Examining the Question

> All questions must be open to scrutiny, and the results must be
> interpreted with great caution.
>   Herbert Spirer, Louise Spirer, and A.J. Jaffe (Spirer, Spirer, and
>   Jaffe, 1998, p. 154)

Have you ever been approached about completing a survey and then become
frustrated about the way the questions were posed? Perhaps the questions did
not address the issues you were most concerned about. Or they did not give
you the best choices for voicing your opinion on a topic. Some third graders felt
the same kind of disenfranchisement when their teacher used a graphing
experience to encourage her students to make healthier choices at snack
time (Whitin, 2006).

She had noticed that although some of her students brought fruit, many
of them also brought chips, cookies, or other, less healthy foods. In order
to emphasize the importance of fruit she decided to conduct a survey about
children's favorite snack, but would only include apples, oranges, grapes or
bananas as the possible choices. Afterwards, one child asked her why she
only included fruits when "a lot of kids bring in different kinds of food for
snack." The teacher admitted that she wanted to focus on healthy snacks and so
purposely did not offer crackers, chips, or cookies.

This child's question highlighted the teacher's motive: she wanted to
develop a classroom culture that valued better nutritional habits. This purpose
was also part of the larger school agenda of supporting healthy eating.
Her status as a teacher gave her power to control the survey choices to promote
her point of view. As critics the children exposed her intentions and argued that
even though the data showed that bananas were the favorite fruit at snack time,
it was not necessarily the favorite snack. The question had positioned them to
respond in a certain way and they voiced important objections to that kind of
verbal manipulation.

We use this example to show that although the data-collection process
might seem to begin with a question, from a critical perspective it does not.
This snack survey began with the motive and status of the teacher and agenda
of the school. By the time questions are posed, they already have a complex
history of personal interests, motives and points of view. Data-related questions, like all forms of communication, arise from particular social com-
munities that have specialized ways of thinking, believing, valuing, and acting

(Gee, 1992, 1999). As we will describe later in this chapter, this fabric of context influences word choice (e.g., "welfare" vs. "assistance to the poor"). It influences phrasing, too, by placing some ideas in the foreground and others in the background. In Gee's words, "Grammar simply does not allow us to speak from no perspective" (1999, p. 4).

In a larger sense, the issue involves who asks the question, what is the time and place, and through what mode is the question posed. The apple graph example in Chapter 1 illustrated that the question involved the physical property of the apples themselves. The aspect "expressive mode" in our model (Figure 1.1) reflects this materiality (Kress, 2000). Other expressive forms of communicating questions yield various kinds of responses (e.g., face-to-face oral questions, phone interviews, paper or digital surveys, and so on).

We argued in Chapter 1 that the social context permeates all parts of the process of collecting, interpreting, and reporting data. Examining these aspects as they relate to "the question" gives them a meaningful context. We will therefore use both sets of questions from our heuristic to guide our discussion (Figure 1.2):

The social context:
- What is your purpose for collecting this information?
- Who is you audience?
- How are you collecting this information?

The question:
- How did you ask your question?
- Why did you ask it in that way?
- How might this language have influenced the responses you received?
- What groups of people did your question privilege? Silence?

How else might the question have been worded? In the following sections we give examples from the media as well as from classrooms to highlight the role of these social influences, as well as aspects of the question itself, such as wording, structure, and mode. Later we will take an in-depth look at a fifth-grade investigation that incorporates many of these ideas.

The Complexity of Simple Questions

Seemingly simple questions can be complex. This realization is an important one for critics to gain because it propels them to look beyond the surface of purported results and examine how choices were made about the wording of the question. By living through this complexity themselves children are less likely to accept the seemingly simple, pat, "unbiased" reports of others. The following examples show how children confronted this issue of complexity and question posing: a fourth grader considers a survey about the bedtimes of her peers; and some fifth-grade children realize that the questions they had written on a paper survey about the school lunch program were not as clear as they thought they were.

Fourth grader Amanda asked her teacher if she could conduct a survey of her friends using the following question: "What time do you have to go to bed?" The teacher had been encouraging the children to create surveys to learn more about their classmates. Amanda proposed this topic because it was an issue in her own household. However, as she thought more about how to exactly phrase the question, she realized the task was going to be more complex than she had first imagined. She explained to her teacher that on Friday and Saturday she stays up later; she also has a later bedtime once or twice a week when she stays overnight at her aunt's house. On the other hand, she shared that sometimes she goes to bed earlier, such as on days when she has soccer practice. This reflection about her own experiences caused her to think how her friends might have similar problems identifying a singular bedtime, as her question was positioning them to do. Amanda finally decided to abandon the topic because of all this potential complexity she saw in trying to pose the question. Her analysis of the possible problems inherent in that question gave her an insider's view of how a question can narrow responses and not capture the full complexity of the topic.

A group of fifth graders discovered that posing questions in a written format has its own set of complexities. In Chapter 1 we introduced children from two classes with whom we worked throughout the year. In January the principal put these classes in charge of gathering data from other students about the strengths and needs of the school lunch program and to report their findings to the school board. To begin the project, the children developed a survey that they administered to one class of third, fourth, sixth, and ninth graders. In order to determine if the cafeteria menu matched the student body's food preferences, the children decided to ask respondents to name favorite foods other than pizza, a known preference. They also wanted to know which students most regularly ate cafeteria lunches since these students would be in the best position to evaluate the program. Therefore, the survey began with these two questions:

1. About how many times a week do you eat school lunch?
   a. 0–1   b. 2–3   c. 4–5
2. What is your favorite:
   a. fruit   _____
   b. vegetable   _____
   c. main dish (not pizza) _____
   d. dessert   _____

When the children began to tabulate the results, they were surprised to find that two of the sixth-grade papers had nothing written in the blank spaces. Instead, one of the choices was circled (e.g., "d" next to "dessert"). "What do you think these children were thinking when they saw #2?" we asked. After some discussion, we all came to the conclusion that the format of the question resembled a multiple-choice test. The idea seemed plausible, especially since students had recently completed the annual state standardized test.

The children wondered if there were other instances of miscommunication in the survey. Jermaine noted that some other surveys had two foods written in the blank spaces rather than just one. "Maybe we should have said, 'your *very* favorite' instead," he suggested. David raised another issue. Since the first question focused the respondents' attention on school lunches, perhaps some of the children interpreted the second question to mean, "What is your favorite cafeteria food?" rather than "What is your overall favorite food?" His comment showed the children how the order of questions can make a difference in the answers one receives. Kenya, who had delivered the survey to the third grade, added that some of the children had asked what "main dish" meant. The children wondered how else that category might have been labeled. As these students discovered, communicating one's intentions through the structure, spatial arrangement, sequence, and wording of written questions is indeed a complex, multimodal matter (Jewett & Kress, 2003). Raising children's awareness of these complexities provides an important foundation for nurturing a critic's perspective toward the question.

Different Questions Yield Different Results

Even slight changes in the wording of a question can produce different responses. In this section we examine how the change of a few words, or the inclusion of a small detail, can affect one's results. Think about the difference between "assistance to the poor" and "welfare." Do they mean the same thing? Apparently not, according to surveys conducted for years by the National Opinion Research Center at the University of Chicago and by the *New York Times*/CBS News Poll (Kagay & Elder, 1992). The first question that was posed to the public was whether or not the United States was spending too much, too little, or about the right amount of money on "assistance to the poor." Two-thirds of the respondents said that the United States was spending too little. However, when the wording was changed from "assistance to the poor" to "welfare," almost half of the respondents said that the United States was spending too much on welfare. Although the wording of each question may seem synonymous to some, for most of the respondents these were two different questions. Words have connotations and people bring their own personal ideologies to bear as they interpret the question. "Welfare" may conjure up a belief in large governmental programs, while "assistance to the poor" may connote a more humanitarian connotation. Thus, the wording of a question involves the ideologies of the surveyors, and two questions about the same issue can produce strikingly different results.

Children themselves need opportunities to witness how two different versions of a question can have a significant impact on the kind of data that is collected. Take the example of Sarah, a second-grade student, who was perturbed about a family policy that did not allow her to go out alone to play with friends in the next courtyard area of her large apartment complex. Sarah asked her teacher if she could conduct a survey on this issue so that she would have some data to support her point of view. This motive for gathering the data helped her shape how she actually posed the question. She discussed the construction of the question with her teacher:

Teacher: How might you ask your question?

Sarah: I could say, "Would you let your kid walk to their friend's house alone?" Or maybe I should say, "Would you let your 9-year-old walk to their friend's alone?"

Teacher: Do you think there would be a difference in people's answers if they knew how far away you lived from your friend's house?

Sarah: So maybe I should say, "Would you let your 9-year-old walk alone to a friend's house which is right around the block?"

As Sarah reread her first question she predicted that a lot of people would probably say "no" because they would not know the age of the child. So she revised it and proposed her second question. Although she was only 8 years old at the time, she reasoned that by including an older age (which she was fast approaching) might be more appealing to her responders. At this point the teacher raised a question about distance and Sarah felt that this detail ought to be included as well. Teachers play an important role in suggesting these kinds of possibilities so that children see that they have many choices in the way they frame the question.

Sarah was now satisfied that the question contained enough specifics to attract the support for her cause. She collected data from 14 adult relatives at a family gathering. After she had asked a few people, some of them began talking among themselves and raising questions such as, "I wondered what time of day it was"; "Where exactly was this taking place?" In fact, one person even changed his answer from a "yes" to a "maybe" since the question did not state the time of day. Her final results were: 12 no, 1 yes, and 1 "maybe." She shared the results with her teacher, and admitted that she was a bit disappointed in them.

After discussing with her teacher the additional questions people raised, her teacher challenged her to think of a way in which she might use this information to revise the question once again. Together they formulated the following question: "If you know the neighborhood is safe and you know your neighbors, would you let your 9-year-old walk alone around the block to a friend's house?" Sarah went home and telephoned other relatives to gather the data a second time. Her new results were: 8 yes, 6 no. When she reported this data to her teacher they talked about how the language of a question can influence the data one receives. Sarah noticed that the more specific the criteria she included in her question, such as being older (9 years), walking nearby (around the block), and being in a safe environment (safe neighborhood), the more likely she would receive the votes she wanted.

Indeed, even young children can build an awareness of how different versions of a question can produce quite different results. We will look here at a kindergarten class in which children were given regular opportunities to collect data from their peers (Whitin, 1997). On the same day two different children collected data about their peers' favorite colors and discovered how their different questions yielded different findings. First, Mark decided to canvass his friends on their favorite color. He wrote the three color words that he knew how to spell, namely red, green, or black, on a piece of paper and asked his friends to indicate which of these colors was their favorite. After interviewing nine of his peers he approached his teacher and said, "Jesse's favorite color is purple, but I don't know how to spell 'purple.' I only know how to spell these." She reminded him to use the color word chart, and he copied these other color words on to another piece of paper: blue, orange, white, purple, yellow, pink, and brown. He offered this new list of words to the remaining seven students but decided not to offer them the three words he had on his original list. He then combined his data and reported to his class the combined results: 3 red, 3 green, 3 black, 3 purple, 2 brown, 1 white, and 0 orange, blue, pink, and yellow.

Later that afternoon Mark's friend, Jamie, decided he wanted to do a color survey too. Mark accompanied Jamie as he went about the task. Jamie chose his own set of colors from the color chart, and reported his own set of findings: 5 red, 5 blue, 3 green, 3 purple, and 0 orange, yellow, brown, and black. The teacher wanted to capitalize on this event to help them see this important relationship between questions and results, so she asked, "Why did you both find different answers for the colors?" Mark admitted that he only offered three choices to his first nine responders, and then offered a different set of choices to the remaining seven responders. Jamie offered the same set of colors to all 16 classmates but he did not offer the same colors as Mark (Jamie omitted red, white, and pink). As they discussed the different decisions that each of them made, the children better understood how different questions about the same topic produce different results.

In these past three examples we have been examining the wording of a question with some attention paid to the motive of the surveyor. Now we want to shift our attention to a more critical analysis of motive, and how questions reflect those motives.

The Motive Influences the Question

Critics ask why a person, company, or organization might have an interest in collecting a set of data. What is their motive? What hidden agenda might they be promoting, and to what extent is that ideology embedded in their data-gathering process? Who is most likely to benefit from obtaining the information in this way? These kinds of questions help to expose the social context of this statistical venture. The example surrounding the issue of gun control in Chapter 1 helps to illustrate how the socio-political factors of differing viewpoints can influence the construction of the survey questions. Specifically, why would the National Rifle Association (NRA) conduct a survey about gun control? What is their motive? Given their agenda of unfettered gun ownership they created a question that would help them promote their particular point of view: "Would you favor or oppose a law giving police the power to decide who may or may not own a firearm?" (Best, 2001, p. 48). Of course, it is not the police who decide this issue; they only enforce the laws passed by state and/or federal government. However, by framing them as the judges of gun ownership, and using the alliterative force of "*giving police the power*" to emphasize this connection, the NRA effectively conjures up images of a police state. They could then use the results of this survey to argue that the vast majority of Americans do not favor any kind of gun control.

On the other hand, advocates for restrictions on gun control, who have their own ideology for protecting the safety of the public, posed this question: "Do you favor cracking down on illegal gun sales?" Given their motive to curb gun sales they framed the question to emphasize the illegality of certain gun transactions. After all, who is not against stopping any kind of illegal activity? Choosing emotionally charged words, such as "illegal," helps to trigger the responses one is seeking. In addition, both of these questions only invited a yes or no response. This binary choice was no accident. Both groups did not want any middle-ground responses that would detract from the stark contrast they were trying to create.

However, depending on one's purposes, an open-ended question might be more useful, but here again motive can play a role in this venture. The Colgate-Palmolive Company used an open-ended question when they asked dentists and hygienists to recommend effective toothpaste. However, the company's failure to disclose the exact wording of the question made their advertising claims appear misleading and deceitful (Derbyshire, 2007). The company claimed in these advertisements that 80% of dentists recommended their toothpaste. The Advertising Standards Authority (ASA) in England banned the company from using this claim after they investigated how the question was actually posed. This telephone survey of dentists and hygienists allowed each dentist to recommend *more than one type of toothpaste*. As a result of this finding the ASA charged the company with misleading consumers: "The claim would be understood by readers to mean that 80% of dentists recommend Colgate over and above other brands, and the remaining 20% would recommend different brands" (Derbyshire, 2007). Instead, Colgate™ was not singled out exclusively by dentists but was one of a group of recommended toothpastes. Critics know the importance of interrogating the question and uncovering motives so they can better evaluate claims based on reported data.

Teachers can support children to develop an awareness of how motives can influence the development of the questions. In one example, Paul, a fourth-grade student, was challenged by his teacher to brainstorm some questions related to an issue that he often complained about, namely his 8 p.m. bedtime. His teacher wanted him to experiment with a range of questions that reflected different points of view. In this way he could gain a deeper understanding of how questions mirror the intentions of the researcher. She began, "Let's experiment with posing a variety of survey questions that you think might get you the data that would support your position." He formulated the following four questions:

1. "What time do you think a fourth-grade honor roll student should have as a bedtime, 8 p.m. or later?" He reasoned that he ought to include the "honor roll" part to show how responsible he was. He was using the status of this recognition to convince others.
2. "Do you think that 8 p.m. is too early to send a child to bed when the sun goes down after 9 p.m.?" Since it was late spring and daylight hours were increasing, he thought of capitalizing on the time of year to bolster his case.
3. "If you are awake anyway, is it OK to stay up for another half hour?" He thought if he named an actual increment of time he would gain at least that specified amount.
4. "Would you increase family time if you could?" Here he strategically co-opted "family time" as an important value to work on his behalf.

In order for Paul to see how questions could be designed for opposing motives, his teacher asked him to think of a question that might be used to undermine his cause. His reply, "Do you believe a good night's sleep is important for a young child?" demonstrated a clear shift in perspective. By challenging children to ask hypothetical questions from several points of view, teachers can help children like Paul to examine questions for their underlying motives.

Further Dimensions of the Social Context

A critical analysis of motive focuses on the intention and status of the researcher. Other social dimensions identified in our model (Figure 1.1) affect the data that is collected as well. People collect data through a wide range of expressive modes: face-to-face, over the phone, on paper, electronically. Place matters as well. The same question posed at a school, a park, or at a sports arena might elicit different answers. As for ideology, examples involving self-reported data sometimes show more about respondents' perceptions of socially acceptable ways of acting than their actual behavior. Two such stories illustrate how aspects of the social context particularly relate to our discussion of "the question."

A team of researchers were interested in investigating differences between people's perceptions of their own moral attitudes and their actions (Carey, 2009). The study comprised two parts. First, pollsters asked 251 students at Cornell University to predict the likelihood of their buying a daffodil in support of an upcoming fund-raising event sponsored by the American Cancer Society. Eighty-three per cent of those surveyed indicated that they would buy at least one daffodil. For comparison, they were also asked to predict other people's level of participation, and their estimated rate dropped to 53%. In this way they showed more confidence in their own level of moral responsibility than they did in those of their peers. When the event actually took place, the results of the sale showed that both of these estimates had been overly optimistic. Instead of 83% or even 53%, a rate of only 43% of the student body participated by buying at least one daffodil to support the cause.

From a socio-cultural perspective, the predictions reflect ways in which people take on the methods of thinking that are deemed "normal" by the groups with whom they identify (Gee, 1992, 1999). These college students' high rate of affirmative predictions reflected their perceptions about the socially favored ways of acting in their community. A group of fifth graders who investigated their peers' attitudes about littering encountered similar effects of self-reported data. We will take an in-depth look at their experiences in order to show how they explored many of the social aspects discussed throughout this chapter.

Designing the Littering Survey

Earlier in this chapter (the lunch survey example) and in Chapter 1 we introduced children from two fifth-grade classes with whom we worked throughout the school year. The "littering survey" related here involved these children as well, and the investigation began the week following the "chores survey." These particular children were respondents to that first survey, and they participated in the follow-up class discussion. This information helps place the littering survey in its context, as does the planning session we had with the teachers, Kristen and Leslie.

We asked the two teachers to suggest topics for data collecting that related to the children's interests or school-related issues. After naming a few—shopping, video games, or soda flavors—Kristen suggested finding a topic that incorporated the school's character education program, such as respect for property. As an example, the teachers explained that the principal stressed the importance of keeping the school litter-free. The school recycled newspapers as a community service and fund-raising project. In addition, there had recently been an instance of graffiti in the rest room, and all upper-grade teachers had discussed this issue with their classes. We agreed that this topic would be a timely and meaningful one.

The motive for this choice bears some similarity to the snack survey in the chapter's opening. Kristen and Leslie saw an opportunity to connect the values espoused by their school to the children's academic work, and their status as teachers enabled them to do so. Like the third graders in the snack survey, these older children examined some of the effects that this motive behind the topic had, or might have had, on their classmates. In contrast to the snack example, however, these fifth graders designed and carried out the survey, and they reflected on various social forces throughout the process.

In retrospect, the children realized that as the designated surveyors they might have gained a high-status role in the eyes of their peers. Kristen and Leslie each chose three children to work with us in designing and conducting the survey. All of the children knew from our work on the chores survey that the project would involve most of the school day. Only children whom the teachers viewed as able to keep up with their required work could participate. Thus, the privileged status of the interviewers, and the amount of time they were excused from class to carry out this task, were important features of the social context that may have influenced their peers' responses.

To begin the investigation, we told the children about their teachers' choice of topic and invited them to tell us about the school's involvement with this effort. They expressed dismay about the graffiti incident, described the recycling program, and noted that the principal set an example by picking up litter in the hallways. David next asked them to brainstorm questions that they might pose to their classmates. They suggested:

- Why do we need to keep the school clean?
- How do you feel when people write on the wall?
- Do you care about school property?
- How could you keep the school clean when people litter?
- What do you think people [visitors] think when they see litter or writing on the wall?
- [Our school] is one of the schools that recycles the most. What if we didn't do that any more? How would you feel?
- How do you feel when outdoor equipment is broken?

Their range of suggestions offered us an opportunity to guide the children in evaluating the structure of a question and to critically consider how their peers might feel when asked different variations of the question. David began by asking the children to identify examples that would only have two answers (yes/no), such as "Do you care about school property?" After they pointed out a few such questions, he continued, "What might people think when they hear this kind of question? How might they feel?" The children were certain that most people would answer "yes," and their explanations showed that they were keenly aware of both the values of the school and their social position as students. As one child explained, "They might lie because they're afraid they might get in trouble." Her choice of the word "trouble" signals her awareness of how a negative response might be interpreted by high-status members of the social community.

David next asked the children to think about the questions that had more than one answer, such as, "How do you think we could make the school cleaner?" Christy suggested that this kind of question would allow people to "tell a reason, so they couldn't lie as much." Brittaney elaborated on Christy's idea. She pointed to "How do people feel when outdoor equipment is broken?" as another example. "People might have different opinions. They might feel bad or guilty, or didn't care about it, like, 'Maybe I don't care because it doesn't belong to me.'" Her ideas sparked a conversation about the range of attitudes that members of the student body probably had about the environment, as well as the level of commitment to the school's agenda of respect for school property. After this discussion, they agreed that phrasing a question in a way that gave the respondents options would yield more reliable results. Collaboratively, they developed a scenario:

> You see garbage on the floor. Would you pick it up? Would you tell them to pick it up? Do the same thing [also litter]? Or do nothing?

Looking it over, Kayla wondered if the word "garbage" would negatively influence those polled because of health considerations. Indeed, cleanliness and good health were also stressed strongly in the school. The group then decided to substitute "candy wrapper" for "garbage." Kayla's insight highlighted for the children how even the choice of one word can impact upon how people respond.

We adults added a suggestion. Since we were going to poll two classes, three children could ask the question as it stood, and the other team could leave the question open-ended, i.e., with no fixed choices. In that way we could see to what extent different structures of the question yielded different results. Thus, the two formats were:

1. If you saw someone drop a candy wrapper on the floor, what would you do? Why?
2. If you saw someone drop a candy wrapper on the floor, what would you do?
   a. ask them to pick it up   b. do the same thing   c. tell a grownup   d. do nothing   e. pick it up yourself

In designing the survey, the children considered the wording and structure of the question, and examined questions from the perspective of the audience. Words such as "garbage" could potentially convey conflicting messages (e.g., health risks) that would interfere with the intent of the question. Like those who analyzed the effect of choosing words such as "assistance to the poor" and "welfare," these children realized that the wording of a question impacts upon data collection. In addition, yes/no questions, those with fixed responses, and open-ended questions could potentially yield very different results, particularly in the case of such a strongly value-laden topic such as littering. Although we did not explicitly guide the children to interrogate the role of status, motive, and the ideology of the school as they related to this investigation, their discussion about those who "might lie" demonstrated their developing awareness about these critical issues. As they conducted, interpreted, and shared results with the classes, additional opportunities arose for the children and their classmates to critique their questions and these social dimensions.

Conducting and Interpreting the Litter Survey

We divided the group into two teams of three children. David's group posed the open-ended version of the question, and Phyllis's group followed the question with the five pre-set choices. One pollster summoned the respondents one at a time to join the team in the hallway. Team members took turns posing the question, and as the respondent spoke, four people—the three children and an adult—wrote down their words. From a critical perspective these contextual aspects of the survey were inextricably connected to the survey question. The respondents were also outnumbered four to one. From a modal perspective, the design of the survey was face-to-face, with questions and responses orally posed, but also recorded in writing. Taken together, these features gave an aura of importance and power to the pollsters and an official tone to the event (Gee, 1999). These aspects were an inherent part of the question. Figure 2.1 summarizes these social aspects.

With these considerations in mind, it was not surprising that both versions of the question yielded similar results: an overwhelming number of children responded that they would pick up the candy wrapper. For the open-ended version, 19 children said that they would pick it up, and four replied that they would ask the person who dropped the wrapper to pick it up. When asked for a reason, they expressed several ideas, as Kayla's notes show (Figure 2.2). David asked his team to examine the reasons, group together similar responses, and name the categories. They identified two categories, grouping together 14 responses such as "It's not right because it is littering" with the label, "about littering", and seven others such as "I'm a tree hugger" as "about the earth's environment." This experience highlighted another difference between open-ended and fixed-response questions. In the case of open-ended questions, categories emerge from the data that are collected.

The results for the fixed-answer choices were:

- Ask the person to pick it up   4
- Do the same thing   0

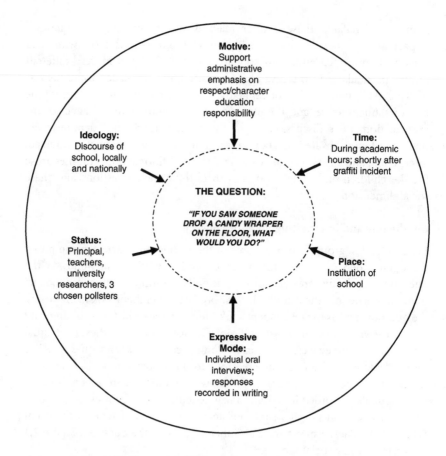

EXAMINING THE SOCIAL CONTEXT OF THE QUESTION

Figure 2.1 Examining the social context of the question, "If you saw someone drop a candy wrapper on the floor, what would you do?"

- Tell a grownup   1
- Do nothing   1
- Pick up the paper   18

Figure 2.3 shows Jackson's graph of their results.

After the children had made their graphs, we asked them to interpret the results and to critique the structure, wording, and presentation of the questions to their peers. Brittaney, one of the fixed-response team, said that their group "didn't let them say what they wanted," implying that the respondents were limited. However, as Phyllis pointed out, the open-ended group's responses yielded only two kinds of answers, namely "pick it up" or "ask them to pick it up," whereas the fixed-response group had four different responses. Jackson then mused, "If we hadn't given the categories, then maybe they wouldn't have

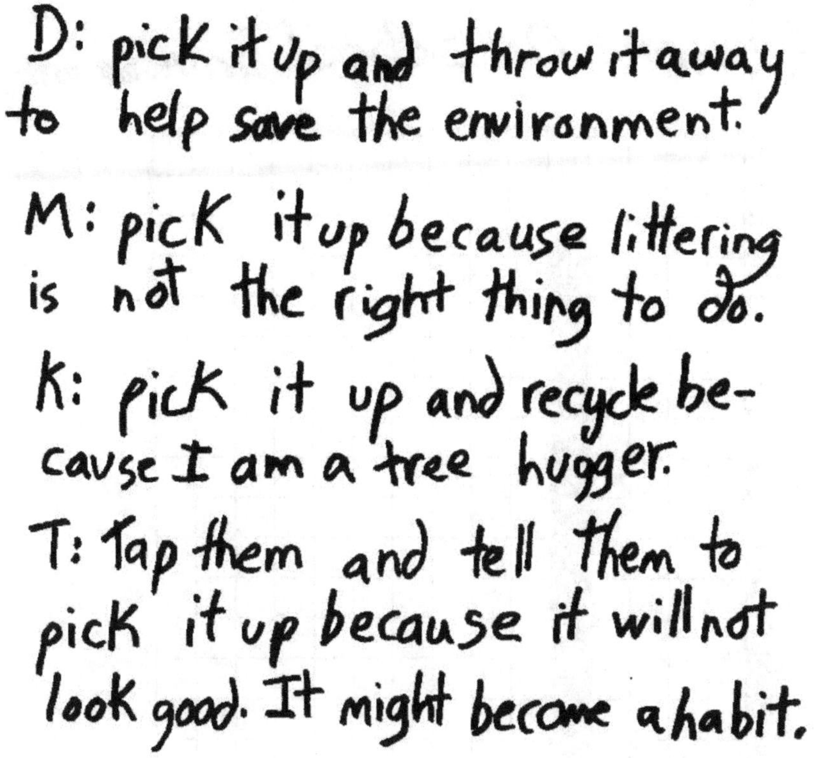

D: pick it up and throw it away to help save the environment.

M: pick it up because littering is not the right thing to do.

K: pick it up and recycle because I am a tree hugger.

T: Tap them and tell them to pick it up because it will not look good. It might become a habit.

Figure 2.2 Notes from data collection showing children's reasons for their littering survey responses.

thought of 'grownups' " [as in "Tell a grownup"]. His point raised an interesting issue. Originally the children had thought that giving an open-ended question would allow for a greater range of responses, but the results caused them to raise doubts about this relationship. Perhaps instead of limiting responses, listing options may have actually prompted children to consider different options. On the other hand, by asking the follow-up question, "Why," the open-ended group did gather more fine-grained responses than the pre-set category group, which they were then able to sort into two subcategories.

Although there was no definitive way to settle the issue of what kind of question was more beneficial, the children were developing insights into the complexity of designing questions as described by Schuman and Scott (1987). These authors note that people are often attracted to the choices offered in a closed survey even when they are given the opportunity to add a choice beyond the list. This finding is an important one from a critic's perspective. Since people take what is offered to them, critics know that power and control resides

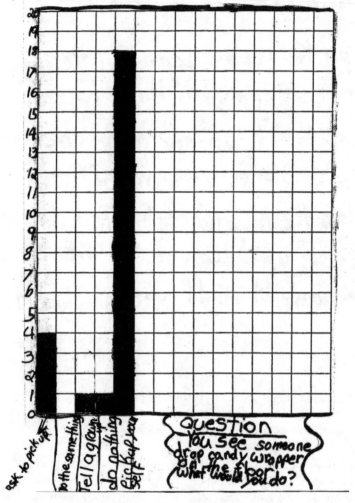

Figure 2.3 Graph of fifth graders' responses to the question: "If you saw someone drop a candy wrapper on the floor, what would you do?"

with those who create those choices. Thus, choosing the format of the question involves trade-offs; there are benefits and limitations to any option.

The high number of the "pick it up" responses turned the children's attention to the larger social context of the survey. They had already considered that students "might lie" about their actions or beliefs, and they now reconsidered this issue based on their experience of conducting and analyzing the survey.

We summarized the conditions under which the question was posed: the respondents were summoned into the hall one at a time; they faced three interviewers who looked very official with their clipboards, and were accompanied by a university professor. We then asked the children to put themselves in the place of those whom they interviewed.

"They might have felt pressure to say it [pick it up] because we were all standing around and writing everything down," observed Christy. "They might be just saying it so they won't get in trouble," added Brittaney. Noting that only one person had said that they would "do nothing," she added, "Maybe 'do nothing' is truthful." Thoughtfully, Jason admitted, "I would probably do nothing. I have to be honest." Putting themselves in their classmates' places helped give the children a new perspective. Thus, in addition to the actual wording and structure of the question, there were social factors in play that may have influenced the kinds of responses the children received. Through this experience, these children began to consider ways in which status and ideology are an integral part of collecting data from other people.

Although the vast majority of "pick it up" responses might be attributed to "feeling pressure," nonetheless, the children were quite sure that at least some of the responses reflected good intentions rather than definitive actions. As Maya pointed out, "Will they *start* doing it [pickup paper], or have they been doing it already?" The fifth graders had discovered for themselves the limits of self-reported data. In their report to the class, the children included their misgivings about the validity of their results. Their teachers suggested that observing what people really do would be a way to gather further data about the issue. Like the study of Cornell students and the daffodils-for-cancer campaign, the fifth graders could conduct a follow-up investigation, by going "under cover to see what kids and teachers *really* do about littering," as Cassandra later described it.

Collecting Follow-up Data: Going "Under Cover"

On our next visit to the school we met with a new group of four children to plan the follow-up investigation. We opened the discussion by reviewing the findings from the first survey and asked for their thoughts. Malik was sure that there was a difference between the way in which children responded and what they would actually do, offering evidence from his experience: "I'm on safety patrol. I see [people 'doing nothing'] every day. People drop candy wrappers on the floor, but I have to ask them to pick it up." We asked them to estimate about how many people would actually pick up a wrapper. Their predictions were very different from the findings of the first survey: Cassandra suggested that 3% of those observed would pick up the wrapper, while Jamar and Tonya suggested that about a quarter would do so. Jamar further predicted that older students would pick up fewer wrappers than younger ones. His comment echoed the sentiments that arose during the whole-class presentations of the oral survey. In fact, one child had commented that the ninth-grade hall is "like a tornado," with a lot of paper strewn on the floor. Here was another similarity between these children's work and the daffodil study at Cornell. Cornell students predicted a higher rate of the socially valued action for themselves than for others, and the fifth graders predicted a higher rate for their own grade level than for the seventh to ninth graders.

Observing students in two different parts of the building offered the children an opportunity to test both of their questions:

- Is there a difference between what children say and what they do?
- Are younger children more conscientious about picking up litter than older children?

Both pairs of observers followed the same procedure: place a piece of crumpled paper in the middle of the hallway, wait out of view by stepping into a doorway, and count the number of people who passed the paper before someone picked it up. They also agreed to note other pertinent information as well (e.g., the approximate grade level or adult role of the person who picked up the paper). They repeated the procedure for as many trials as possible within the designated half-hour observation period.

We were all very surprised by the results. Tonya and Cassandra, who watched passers-by in the fourth- and fifth-grade hall, conducted five trials, and in all but one case an adult picked up the paper. One teacher caught sight of Tonya and directed her to pick up the paper. Interestingly, the principal was the first to stop for the litter, responding after 23 others had passed by. In the other trials a range of 17 to 195 people passed by. The girls were amazed that not one student retrieved the paper, even though Kristen's entire class filed by on the way to lunch. These results were indeed different from those from the self-reported data collected the previous week!

Malik and Jamar, along with David, recorded three trials as they watched seventh, eighth, and ninth graders on their way to the cafeteria for lunch. They were momentarily distracted and missed the opportunity to identify who picked up the paper for the first trial (after 27 people). They next counted 73 people who passed the paper before an adult picked it up. For the final trial 60 people passed, and a ninth grader removed the paper. These results caused the children to question their preconceived notions about older students' level of responsibility. Even though the number of trials was very small, they wondered if their hypothesis about older students was really accurate.

We broke for lunch after the children collected their data. When we reassembled, Tonya, who was a member of Kristen's class, reported that she had told her friends about their secret data collection. They insisted that they had not seen the paper. As the four children considered this new information, we raised the point that most of the students came through the hall with their classes, and teachers expected children to "stay in line," so a child might be reluctant to stop and pick up the paper. On the other hand, Tonya and Cassandra were sure that at least some of the adults had been aware of the paper. They noted that on two occasions adults stepped on the paper while walking alone, but they did not stop to pick it up. They interpreted this observation as evidence that these people ignored the paper because they would have heard it or felt it. Considering these additional points helped the children to see that like all data-collecting endeavors, this investigation was not context-free. Despite these uncertainties, however, the children realized that the overwhelming difference between the two investigations made a strong case that self-reported data can be unreliable.

As the children prepared their summary reports for their classmates, they agreed to avoid words such as "lying" that would sound accusatory about the discrepancy between the results of the first and second survey. In the conclusion to her written report, Tonya noted that when asked the question in the first survey, most students in her class had said they would pick up the paper, "but they didn't [pick it up in the hallway]. We think you felt pressure. It's okay to feel pressure." When she showed her graph to her peers, she pointed to the various bars representing the number of people who had passed by, but also told them about the lunch conversation with her friends. "So," she added, "on the graph you *can't tell* who saw [the paper] and who didn't." The sensitivity that these children showed for their classmates' feeling "pressured" demonstrated their developing awareness of the ways in which aspects of the social context permeate a question's implied messages. The question on the first survey, "If you saw a candy wrapper on the floor, what would you do?" entailed much more than words. As a survey conducted within the school setting, it involved the "pressure" to act according to ways that are socially defined as "normal" for reputation and membership in the school community. Posing the questions orally and outnumbering the respondents further accentuated this agenda. Like the Cornell students in the daffodil study, these children were reluctant to appear as going against the perceived social norms of their community (Gee, 1992, 1996).

Next Steps: Strategies for Critiquing the Questions

Critics need regular opportunities to examine how the wording of the question, as well as the conditions under which it is created and posed, affect the results one receives. The examples in this chapter point to some classroom strategies that teachers might employ:

- *In what way can children's interests and experiences be a foundation for them to brainstorm a range of questions that reflect varying motives and ideologies?* Children might test out these different questions and then examine possible links among motive, question and results.

- *What are particular issues and topics children can use for posing both open and closed questions? What are the advantages and disadvantages that they see in each form?*
- Children can test out questions in a preliminary survey. *What do they learn from this initial poll, and how do those insights inform their next revisions? How do the results of the revised questions compare to the original questions?*
- *In what ways can children pose questions to audiences who have varied experiences with the topic? How do children adapt the wording of the question to match this range of experiential backgrounds?*
- *To what extent do survey results vary when children survey peers vs. younger children or older children? Is there evidence that the status of older children has an effect on the results?*
- Children can examine data reports in media sources related to their age and interest and ask, *"What are different possible interpretations of that question? How else could they have asked that question?"*
- Children might create a list of words about a topic that conjure up different connotations (Do we use "garbage" or "litter?"). *How do certain words raise particular feelings, emotions, or attitudes?*
- *How might children investigate the dubious nature of self-reported data? What are topics they could ask their peers about, and then how might they actually observe their peers in action? How does what one says differ from what one does?*

3
Definitions and Categories
Deciding What Gets Counted

> For every complex problem there is an answer that is clear, simple and wrong.
>
> —H. L. Mencken (in Winerip, 2006, p. 154)

One third-grade teacher planned an experiment for his students to determine which popcorn had the better rate of popped kernels: a generic brand or a name brand (Orville's). The experiment seemed simple enough: heat up each one and then observe how many kernels were popped and not popped for each brand. However, once the popping was over the problems of definitions began. "That one's not popped," claimed one child as she pointed to one kernel that was only partially popped. "Yes it is," countered another child, "I would eat it." "Not me, I wouldn't eat one like that," the other student argued. So the criterion of edibility entered the discussion. It counts as "popped" if someone would eat it. But the children soon realized that different children had different ideas about what they would eat and not eat. They finally decided to refine their definition of "popped" as "being popped at least half or more." However, even with that definition the children soon realized that not everyone agreed. Some would eat pieces that were popped even less, and other children would eat only pieces that were fully popped. Nevertheless, given this definition the children found that the generic brand was the "better" popcorn.

However, Orville might challenge the children's definition of what to count and not to count. This company might have asked for data comparing only the number of fully popped kernels, arguing that "fully popped" is a better criterion for defining what is a "better" popcorn. This category of "fully popped" was lost when it was aggregated with the "partially popped." Orville might also argue that "taste" is a more important criterion for determining which is the "better" popcorn. Thus, what began as a seemingly simple science experiment turned into a complex issue about language, definitions and categories.

It is through experiences such as these that children learn that whenever a number is associated with a word (e.g., 157 kernels "popped"), there is a definition lurking in the background that determined what was to be counted. Such experiences also demonstrate to children that numbers are inextricably woven together with language and that this relationship needs to be interrogated. In addition, children realize that behind what appears to be a clean-cut, polished number is the messy reality of conflicting viewpoints and opinions regarding

41

definitions and categories. Children are learning that there are limitations to their purported results because of the definitions they choose to use. In short, everything hinges on the definitions and categories. Voltaire recognized this importance when he once said, "If you wish to converse with me, define your terms" (Spirer, Spirer, & Jaffe, 1998, p.37). Children who grapple with data themselves can appreciate the import of Voltaire's demand.

Definitions carry far-reaching ramifications in social and political contexts. Implications for varying definitions for "homelessness" were briefly discussed in Chapter 1. For more than 20 years the federal government has defined it as the number of people who show up at shelters or who are living in the streets. However, there is continual debate in both the House and Senate about expanding that definition (Swarns, 2008). Advocates for an expanded definition argue that children and families who do not have stable living conditions ought to be counted (estimated to be about one million people). Other legislators propose a more conservative expansion by including only those people who had to leave their homes owing to domestic violence, and those who can verify that they will lose their current housing within 14 days. Another even more narrow definition would include only people who had to move three times within one year, or twice in 21 days. How one defines the problem determines how one does the counting. For those who feel it is the moral obligation of the government to help those in need, the definition ought to be quite broad; for other legislators who feel that this issue is not as serious a problem as others make it out to be, and that any such spending smacks of a socialist government, the definition ought to be as narrow as possible. Definitions can minimize or maximize the magnitude of a problem because socio-political agendas are embedded within this issue of language (Gee, 1996). As a result, choices are made, and there are inevitably winners and losers. Barney Frank, Democrat from Massachusetts and Chair of the House Financial Services Committee, admitted that with limited financial resources, the definition that is finally agreed upon will exclude certain groups of people from assistance: "When there's not enough money to cover 'all of the above,' you have to do priorities. The question is, Which category of people are you going to leave unhelped?" (Swarns, 2008, p.A15).

These two stories underscore how pervasive definitions and categories are in shaping how we view the world. The stories also show how issues of language affect the data we report, and the data we report affect the language we use to discuss and interpret an issue. Once the government decides on the definition of "homeless" then that definition determines what is to be counted. And once these data are reported, the problem of homelessness is minimized or dramatized depending upon how narrow or broad the definition.

Definitions guide the data collecting, which in turn guides the discussion of the particular issue. However, once numbers are tabulated and associated with a word or term, the numerical part of the discussion often overshadows these important issues of language. People are often more reluctant to challenge the numbers, and so the words are left unquestioned as well. As a result people lapse into assuming that everyone shares the same definitions (Gee, 1996). And when people start to assume then they stop questioning. Words such as "school achievement," "research-based results," and "school dropouts" go unquestioned because people assume that they know what these words mean, when in fact others have defined the words for us; and whoever owns the words owns the world. The role of the critic is to challenge, interrogate, and disrupt the normalized definitions of those taken-for-granted words. In this way critics can open up issues for re-examination (Janks, 2010).

In this chapter we examine this interplay of language and mathematics as it relates to the definitions and categories of any data-gathering venture. People create definitions to guide them in deciding what to count (e.g., a homeless person or a popped kernel of corn). Definitions set the parameters for what is to be counted. For instance, in Chapter 1 the fifth graders wondered if bringing one's dishes into the kitchen was a "chore" or just part of a family "routine." The process of defining terms continues as people label categories of data. The decisions that are made about which categories to use, omit, or combine play a significant role in obfuscating some relationships and clarifying others. For this reason skeptics need to pose questions about both of these terms.

Definitions:
- How did you define this word?
- Why did you define it in this way rather than another way?
- What groups of people were privileged or silenced by this definition?

Categories:
- How were the categories decided upon?
- What happened to responses that did not fit into these categories?
- In what other ways might you categorize these data?
- What information is lost by using these categories?

To illustrate these points we use a variety of examples from children as well as the media to show how these human decisions influence the reported results. Although these stories involve both definitions and categories, the first examples particularly highlight definitions while the latter focus more attention on categories. We begin by examining examples of industrial and political statistics. We then show how even young children can grapple with how the narrowing or broadening of a definition can silence some students and give voice to others. An examination of ranking systems raises similar issues. Depending on criteria that people have selected as the most significant, these systems privilege some points of view and marginalize others.

We turn next to other aspects related to categories. We describe how some fifth-grade students experienced the tension of deciding how general or specific categories need to be when they confront unexpected survey responses. We continue with the related issue of how aggregating and disaggregating categories of data reveals and/or conceals relationships and thus can be fashioned to favor a particular point of view. We conclude the chapter with a story in which children use their experiential knowledge to critique categories on a professional agency's survey instrument.

The Role of Categories in Official Statistics

In order to underscore the serious and pervasive impact of definitions and categories, we first share some examples from political contexts. To begin with, we turn to the roots of the No Child Left Behind (NCLB) legislation, which was based on the results of the so-called "Texas miracle" in the Houston public schools. However, this miracle was really a "Texas manipulation" owing to the way in which the district chose to define "dropouts." Houston had touted its dropout rate as only 1.5%, and boasted that it had successfully met the strict standards of the Texas testing system. In addition, it had accomplished all these feats with very little extra funding. However, it was later exposed by both the *New York Times* and CBS News that things were not as they had at first seemed (Wood, 2004). For example, at Sharpston High School 463 of its 1,700 students left during the 2001 to 2002 school year but the school did not report a single dropout. Instead, the school claimed that those students should not be counted as dropouts because "they had changed schools, gone for a G.E.D., or returned to their native country—when many of them never told the school authorities any such thing. In reality the dropout rate in Houston is thought to be somewhere between 33 and 50%" (Wood, 2004, p.36). Thus a "miracle" becomes a "mirage" when skeptics look closely at the definition.

Many would argue that the government's definition of "unemployment" presents a misleading picture of the nation's economy (Leonhardt, 2008). The government counts the "unemployed" as those who do not have a job, have been actively looking for a job in the previous four weeks, and are currently available for work. Many argue that this definition is too narrow and does not accurately reflect the true extent of this problem. For instance, some would claim that the definition ought to include those workers who are working part-time but who want full-time work. Others complain that this definition should include people who have given up trying to find a job.

The famous "ketchupgate" controversy during the Reagan administration provides our final example of attempted political chicanery with definitions. In 1981 the United States Department of Agriculture Food and Drug Administration proposed reclassifying both ketchup and pickle relish from condiments to a vegetable (*New York Times*, 1989). This change would have allowed schools to cut out a serving of cooked or fresh vegetables from its daily nutritional requirements for a hot lunch program. Although the administration argued that this reclassification was meant to address the problem of "plate waste" it also estimated that such a change would save US$1 billion in savings in the cost of meals for low-income students. This proposal was heavily criticized by Congress and was quickly withdrawn by the administration. Had the "vegetable" definition prevailed, children's nutrition would have been compromised.

Included or Excluded? Young Children Discover that Definitions Count

We will turn now to examples in which children explore issues of fairness and equitable representation through their own definitions. In the first story a child decided to show a range of abilities of his classmates. The surveyor in the second story decided against such gradations of competence, much to the dismay of his peers.

Harold was a student in a public preschool program (Whitin, 1997). His teacher often invited the children to conduct a graph about topics of interest. On one particular day Harold told his teacher that he wanted to find out how many of his classmates knew how to tie their shoelaces. This question was certainly an appropriate one to pose, since Harold and his classmates had been practicing for several months trying to learn this skill on a large shoe in the classroom. Harold himself had learned the skill and he was curious to know about the skill level of the others. His knowledge of this skill also influenced how he decided to create the categories for his data. He knew that the first step in the process was crossing the laces, and the second step involved making the loops. To collect his data he asked each person to untie the laces of one of their shoes and then retie it. He carefully watched each person, decided how far along each was in the process, and then noted their expertise on his paper. Since Harold was just learning to write his name he chose to use an "H" (as well as an X) to represent children who knew how to tie their shoelaces. He used a loop and a "C" shape to represent students who could make a loop with the laces. He unexpectedly encountered one student who refused to participate in his survey, and he decided to record that event by placing a "0" on his paper.

From a skeptic's perspective Harold was demonstrating some admirable dispositions. First, he asked each of his classmates to *show* him their ability rather than *tell* him. He knew there was a difference between what people say and what people do. Second, he knew that shoelace tying was not an all-or-nothing affair. There were gradations of ability and he wanted to be sure that his categories reflected that range of expertise. Harold's classmates appreciated the fact that their partial competence was recorded.

In contrast, fellow classmates in a first-grade class were not pleased with the way their abilities were represented. This second story involves Matt, a student who loved riding his new bike (Whitin, Mills, & O'Keefe, 1990). He came in one morning, bubbling with excitement about all the tricks he could perform on his bike. His teacher was struck by his enthusiasm and asked, "You know so much about bikes, Matt. Why don't you conduct a survey and ask your friends a question about bikes?" He thought for a few seconds, and then piped up excitedly, "I know. I'll ask them if they know how to fix bikes!" He grabbed one of the official data-gathering clipboards and off he went to canvass his peers. Like Harold, Matt encountered some unexpected responses because several classmates did not respond with a yes/no answer. One child told him, "I can fix the bike a little bit"; another said, "I don't know how to fix all of it, but I can fix the wheels." Others mentioned they could fix the seat or the handlebars. Matt decided to record all of these responses as "no's" on his tally sheet.

When Matt shared his results at the morning meeting he reported that 14 people could not fix bikes and only seven could. However, some people questioned his criteria for determining his "yes" and "no" categories. One child asked, "I told you I could fix the seat but you wrote down a 'no.' Why did you do that?" A few other students chimed in with similar complaints. Finally Matt proclaimed defensively, "You have to fix all of the bike!" Children with partial expertise were not pleased with his justification. They were especially miffed because they had been lumped together with those who could not fix the bike at all. They felt like disenfranchised citizens whose vote never really got counted and they argued that they needed their own category for those who "can fix some of the bike." They were demanding that their silenced voices be heard. Although Matt remained firm in his decision, this important issue about definitions and categories was raised. Thus, the children in Matt's class were assuming the role of critics by uncovering the definitions of the categories, proposing an alternative way to categorize the data, and claiming that the results would be quite different if the categories had been expanded. Narrowing or broadening the categories can give voice to some and silence others. Here again, data are marked by the fingers of storytellers who want to give their perspective on a particular issue or event.

Questioning the Criteria of Ranking Systems

The public is inundated by rankings on a daily basis: the most livable cities, the best places to retire, the best pizza, and so on. All ranking systems are based on a set of criteria that people have created to define what constitutes "the best." The "best places to retire" might include cultural opportunities, weather, affordable health care, number of golf courses, and so on. Of course, this definition is open to debate. For instance, Jacksonville, Florida might be ranked high on this list. Yet some may argue that its ranking is much too high: the cultural opportunities there are too few, the weather is too humid, and the number of golf courses is irrelevant. So skeptics ask questions about the criteria for any ranking system. Only then can they better understand and evaluate the purported results. We continue this discussion by sharing two sports-related ranking systems and offer the topic of high school rankings as another one for investigation.

Different countries participating in the Olympic Games use various criteria to rank levels of achievement. Borasi (1989) suggests that a valuable exercise for children is to think about alternative ways those rankings could be determined. Some of her suggested criteria include: (1) the quality of the medals won (e.g., the number of gold medals, then silver, then bronze); (2) the quantity of medals (e.g., the total number of medals won); (3) a weighted score, where certain points are assigned to each kind of medal; (4) the ratio of number of medals compared to the country's population, since larger nations have a greater chance of producing more winning athletes; (5) the amount of financial support a country gives to its athletes. All of these alternative definitions for Olympic achievement offer plausible justifications. Brainstorming these various definitions helps to show that "mathematics is not a neutral or controversy-free discipline" (Borasi, 1989, p. 47).

To explore these alternative definitions through the "purposeful, engaging, and social" avenue of drama (Wilhelm, 2006, p. 74), we suggest incorporating role-playing with Borasi's activity. Individuals or pairs of students could assume the role of spokespeople for various participating countries. After researching pertinent demographic statistics for "their" countries, as well as the medal count from the most recent Games, they could devise the most favorable ranking system for their particular country. In a class forum, each country's representatives would present their proposals and entertain the views of others. By examining these varied ranking systems in role, students are likely to gain a more personalized view of the perspectives of less wealthy or powerful nations.

Evan, a fifth-grade student, investigated another sports-related ranking system when he became interested in how the National Basketball Association determined the Most Valuable Player Award. His teacher challenged him to create some ratings himself to see what results he might obtain with each alternative. He felt that the most important criteria were points per game, field goal percentage, and rebounds. His teacher raised other possibilities for him to consider. "Are these the only statistics that represent a player's contribution to the team? What about the number of assists? Or the number of minutes a player was in the game? Or what about the number of fouls a player committed? That part of a player's game would hurt the team." After considering these possibilities, Evan finally decided to add the criteria of assists, free throw percentage, and number of fouls committed to his original list. By revising his criteria he saw how the definition of "most valuable player" can change based on one's personal criteria. Next, his teacher challenged him further by asking if all these criteria were of the same importance. He immediately responded, "No way. Points per game and field goal percentage are the most important." However, he was not sure how to incorporate this idea into his rating system, so the teacher suggested a weighted system where certain criteria received more points than others. Once these points were established, Evan looked at different players from each team and finally determined that Kevin Garnett deserved to win the award.

Although he wasn't surprised by his results, Evan raised questions about one aspect of his investigation. He noticed that some statistics were so close that it seemed unfair to assign them different weighted scores. As an example, Richard Hamilton had a field goal percentage of .529 and Kevin Garnett had a percentage of .525. Evan wondered whether he should have revised his point system in cases where the statistics were especially close. As he rethought this process, his teacher raised yet another issue for him to consider: "Your criteria don't include *when* the points are scored. Isn't it more important for a player to score points when his team really needs them versus when their team is already winning by a lot?" Evan was intrigued by this criterion of "clutch points" and wondered how that statistic (if he could find it) might influence his results. By his teacher playing the role of devil's advocate and raising these alternative perspectives, Evan was able to experience the messy reality of ranking systems and understand that ratings are based on one person's view of what is important.

As a final example, older students might investigate the controversies surrounding *Newsweek*'s list of America's Best High Schools (Winerip, 2006). This ranking is based on a single criterion: the number of Advanced Placement tests taken by students at a high school divided by the number of graduating seniors. The scores that students actually receive on the tests are not figured into the ranking. The *Newsweek* rankings are often in direct opposition to the rankings conducted by state officials, who typically take into account at least a dozen measures of performance, such as student/teacher ratios, qualifications of teachers, available resources for minorities, etc.

For instance, Hillsborough High in Tampa was ranked by *Newsweek* as 21st best school in America, and Pensacola High as 38th best, but both schools received a "D" rating from the state of Florida. At both of these schools only 15 to 20% of Black and Hispanic children read at grade level. This simplistic system by *Newsweek* masks the numerous inequities that exist in public schools. Many people are suspicious that *Newsweek* is merely using this ranking to sell magazines. *Newsweek* is well aware of the popularity of the annual Best Colleges list produced by *U.S. News & World Report* (another list that has many critics). Even Jay Mathews, the creator of this ranking system for *Newsweek*, admitted that his list is a money maker: "I know last year's issue sold very well and that's why we did it again" (Winerip, 2006). He argues that the simplicity of the definition for "Best High Schools" was what was attractive: "It [the definition] is meant to be narrow so people will understand what I am measuring and can decide if it makes sense. Even if most people disagree, I'm delighted that we are having this debate." In response to this praise for simplicity Les Perelman, a director of undergraduate writing at M.I.T., quoted H. L. Mencken: "For every complex problem there is an answer that is clear, simple and wrong"

(Winerip, 2006). In the case of *Newsweek*, rankings are used to sensationalize, stir up debate, and create a cash cow for the magazine. As always skeptics need to employ ever-vigilant scrutiny and interrogation before deciding on the merits of any ranking system.

Grappling with the Complexities of Categorizing Data

Children involved with the popcorn, shoelace-tying, and bike repair investigations all faced the dilemma of what to do with the unexpected response: partially popped kernels, a child who refused to tie a shoelace, and responses such as, "I can fix the seat" instead of "yes" or "no." We have found that during data-gathering classroom endeavors, such ambiguities almost always arise. What to do with the unexpected response is an especially rich context for developing a critical orientation toward data, and the real learning occurs when the responsibility for solving the problems is placed in the hands of children.

In Chapter 2 we described how the fifth-grade children came to realize that some questions in their school lunch survey may have confused some of the fourth-, sixth-, and ninth-grade respondents. We will pick up the story of their analysis of that survey and relate the challenges that the children faced as they tabulated the choices named in the question:

What is your favorite: Vegetable? _____
                            Fruit? _____
                            Main dish? _____
                            Dessert? _____

The children faced numerous problems almost immediately. Some of the questions were easy to resolve. For example, Jermaine found one survey with "jell-o" written in the "fruit" space. "Is jell-o a fruit?" he wondered, and then continued, "Sometimes jell-o has fruit in it." However, Shaun insisted, "Jell-o is a dessert," and they agreed to discount the response. What about the child who wrote "naco" for "main dish?" Was the intended response "nachos" or "tacos?" The children decided it was unfair to ignore this response altogether. This child deserved to be represented in the report, they reasoned, and they added a tally to both categories. To them it was more important to preserve the child's voice, even though they realized that this initial tally had now become two.

An even more complex decision arose from the unexpected responses related to "chicken" for a main dish. Several responses noted "chicken nuggets" while others stated, "chicken." Maya and Randy, the children tallying this part of the survey, decided that nuggets are more of a fast food and needed to be counted in a separate category. Other responses specified the different kinds of preparation of chicken (e.g., "fried chicken," "parmesan chicken," or "barbecue chicken"), which they included in the "chicken" category. Next came "hot wings." Should it be in a category of its own, like chicken nuggets? After some deliberation, they resolved the issue by placing it with "chicken" on the basis that "it's in the 'chicken' family."

Making these decisions highlighted for the children a key tension in creating data reports. Their overriding concern was to convey to the school board information that would improve the lunch program and accurately reflect the student body's preferences. Chicken was mentioned most frequently in the students' responses to "favorite main dish." Grouping together the various preparation choices would give chicken a greater impact to the audience. The way of categorizing helped them best fit form to purpose in order to make their most convincing argument. As one child remarked, "You have to take out some details so that people can focus on the main things more than the details." Still, the children were uncomfortable with sacrificing individual choices, realizing that "not everyone likes the same kind of chicken." There was no simple solution to this complex endeavor. Choices had to be made, and some information would inevitably be lost in the process.

Later, when they prepared their final report, the children did include a graph that showed "chicken" as a favorite. However, they stated in an accompanying bullet point, "The category 'chicken' includes different types of preparations of chicken." In order to give fair representation to the diverse responses of their peers, they expanded on this point with their oral narration, "Chicken varieties included barbecue chicken, grilled or fried chicken, and chicken sandwiches." Thus, these experiences gave the children a heightened awareness of the tension between making categories that are broad enough to show differences, yet narrow enough to include pertinent details.

Aggregated and Disaggregated Data: A Pervasive Issue

The fifth graders chose to group together or aggregate their data to make the report clear and accessible to their audience. However, the choice to aggregate or disaggregate categories reflects bias rooted in the motive of the authors. Critics know to ask questions about these grouping decisions in order to expose motives, uncover bias, and raise alternative interpretations. We will open this discussion with two examples from the published media. Next we will turn to two examples that involve fourth- and fifth-grade children as they confront parallel issues in their own data reports. These stories demonstrate additional dimensions of the teacher's role in capitalizing on children's "insider's views" of categories in order to equip them with a perspective to critique published surveys and data reports.

A *New York Times* article (Saul, 2008) about a lawsuit against the pharmaceutical giant Pfizer demonstrates how combining or aggregating datasets can hide information that works against the interests of the sponsoring agency. One of the plaintiffs' charges involved the marketing of the epilepsy drug Neurontin for the treatment of other ailments, such as pain associated with long-term diabetes. Although Pfizer hired researchers to conduct studies of the extended use of the drug, the earliest study yielded negative results. However, the results were not published for several years. In the interim period, Pfizer funded two studies that produced more favorable results. Eventually, the report that was made public "bundled" (or aggregated) the three studies, thus diluting the negative findings and enabling Pfizer to state that extended use of the drug was effective. Thus, aggregating these studies benefited the drug company and prevented consumers from making more informed decisions about their health care.

An example from the airline industry further highlights how aggregating or disaggregating data can privilege some groups, but silence or disempower others. An article from the *Wall Street Journal* (McCartney, 2007) describes statistical reports about on-time arrivals, flight delays and cancellations, and baggage handling. In this case, the issue of aggregating or disaggregating data involves the decisions on how to report data from both the mainline carriers and their regional affiliates. The U.S. Department of Transportation does not require that these data be presented as aggregates. In their view, reporting statistics in a disaggregated form (i.e., mainline and regional carriers as separate entities) gives specific information that benefits consumers.

Not everyone agrees with the DOT policy. A look at different presentations of the same data helps illustrate why. The February 2007 DOT report gave the on-time arrival rate of 76% for Delta AirLines, Inc. (The definition of "on-time" includes flights arriving within 15 minutes of the scheduled time.) However, two of Delta's biggest regional partners reported much less favorable rates: 53.5% for Comair, and 66.5% for Atlantic Southeast. If the data for Delta and its regional airlines were combined, the overall percentage drops by 13.3%, to 66.5%, thus casting Delta in a less favorable light. Obviously, most Delta officials are quite content with the DOT policy, which does *not* include these regional airlines in the Delta on-time arrival rate.

However, many of the regional affiliates feel quite differently. They argue that the data should be presented as an aggregate because it would bring to light a problem that Delta is trying to hide, namely that their lower on-time arrival rates are the result of Delta's power and control over the regional airlines' schedules. For example, in the aftermath of bad weather, larger planes are often the first to resume flying so that the greatest number of passengers can be accommodated. As a result the regional planes are delayed, and their on-time record suffers. In the view of these regional partners, the disaggregated data exonerates the mainline carriers from taking the responsibility for the decisions that result in the delays of these affiliate airlines. From this point of view, the regional partners are unfairly positioned by the practice of presenting the data in a disaggregated form. Given the industry's use of the data for marketing purposes, consumers may suffer as well. Aggregating or disaggregating categories of data make it possible to tell different stories, promote various agendas, and privilege or marginalize groups of people.

Exploring How Aggregated and Disaggregated Data Conveys Different Messages

Children can develop an understanding about the effects of aggregating and disaggregating data by examining alternative ways to present numerical information. Such insights are more likely to emerge when the topic is tied to the children's interests and experiences. Jeremy, a fourth-grade student, learned about the implications of aggregating and disaggregating data when he conducted a survey about required school uniforms, a policy that he personally did not favor (Whitin, 2006). He had told his teacher, "I think it should be our choice. It's our clothing, and I think we should get to decide whether to wear that or some other clothing." Jeremy interviewed 10 adults and 10 children during "Kids Club," a before- and after-school child care program. He found that eight students disliked uniforms and two preferred them; four adults disliked them and six preferred them. He used PowerPoint software to represent his results (Figure 3.1). He displayed the data for both adults and children, and summarized his findings to his teacher, Stacey, in this way: "Most kids don't want uniforms. Most adults did want them. And most people altogether would not want uniforms because 12 people [kids and adults] did not want uniforms and eight did." Figure 3.2 illustrates how these aggregated data could have been represented. Stacey saw the opportunity to help Jeremy discover how different people might take these same data and display only selected portions of it to

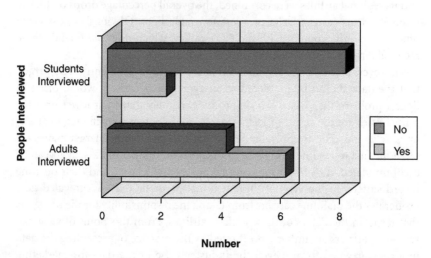

Should All Students Wear Uniforms?

Figure 3.1 Graph showing data from the school uniform survey disaggregated by age. Reprinted with permission from *Thinking and reasoning with data and chance: sixtyeighth yearbook,* copyright 2006 by the National Council of Teachers of Mathematics. All rights reserved.

Should All Students Wear Uniforms?

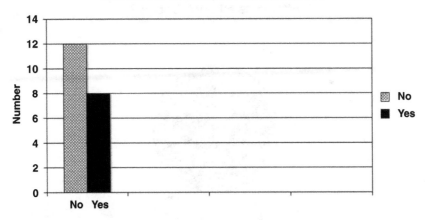

Figure 3.2 Alternate graph showing aggregated data from the school uniform survey.

promote their own point of view. She asked, "How might adults use your data to promote their point of view?" Jeremy admitted that they could disaggregate the student responses and only report the adult ones but that "wouldn't be fair. They aren't showing all the information." By raising this alternative possibility Stacey helped Jeremy see that people can tell very different stories by aggregating and disaggregating data in different ways.

A similar issue arose during the fifth-grade school lunch study described above. The cafeteria director told the children that she was exploring the idea of offering an alternative to the standard hot menu: an option for sandwich, soup, and/or salad. The fifth graders agreed that this change would improve the lunch program. Knowing that they could use data to lobby for the adoption of this option, they decided to include the question, "Would you like to have a choice between the regular lunch OR salad, soup, or sandwich?" on a survey given to third-, fifth-, and eighth-grade classes. They intended to combine the data from all three grades. However, unanticipated questions arose about this decision when Brittaney and Maya, the two in charge of this part of the report, tabulated and graphed the results:

Grade 3	18 yes	6 no
Grade 5	19 yes	1 no
Grade 8	19 yes	2 no
Total	56 yes	9 no

Although the number of "yes" votes was substantial, the girls were surprised that there were nine negative votes. Proceeding with their plan to graph the combined results, they entered 56 and 9 on an Excel sheet and created a pie chart (Figure 3.3). The resulting graph showed 86% "yes" and 14% "no." Since they had originally anticipated nearly 100% "yes," they found this graph to be a

Should Soup/Salad and/or Sandwich Be offered as a Lunch Choice?

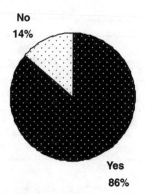

Figure 3.3 Graph showing data from the soup/salad/sandwich survey question with aggregated responses from grades 3, 5, 8.

little disappointing. We adults decided to capitalize on the opportunity to explore aggregated and disaggregated data and drew the girls' attention to the six negative third grade votes. "It's interesting that out of the nine 'no' votes, six of them are from third graders. What do you think about that?" Phyllis asked. Brittaney and Maya recalled that in earlier discussions with their peers, most of the fifth graders had described personal experience with similar menu options when they were in third grade. (It was later discontinued.) With this thought in mind, the girls realized that the current third graders might not have any experience with this kind of option. In fact, they also recalled when the survey was administered that several of the third graders had asked questions about what the choices meant.

With these doubts raised, Phyllis suggested constructing an alternative pie chart that excluded the third graders. Maya and Brittaney agreed and created Figure 3.4. They felt that the results were even more striking: 93% yes and 7% no. Since they did not want to omit the third-grade data entirely they decided to include both graphs in the final PowerPoint report that was shared with the principal, school board, and the cafeteria vendor. They first showed the graph that reflected all three grades (86% yes, 14% no). They included comments on the second graph that explained their reasoning for its inclusion: "Maybe the third graders didn't have experience with a sandwich/salad/soup choice, but some of the older children used to have a choice. Maybe they didn't understand the question. Without the 3rd grade, the no's changed by 7%; 93% said yes to the choice." In this way Brittaney and Maya made their thinking explicit. The girls' choice of the word "maybe" emphasized that their conclusions were hypothetical and tentative. Thus these unanticipated survey results

Lunch Choice Question Grades 5 and 8 Only

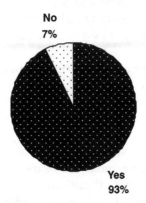

No
7%

Yes
93%

Figure 3.4 Graph showing data from the soup/salad/sandwich survey question without the third grade responses.

gave the girls and their peers opportunities to discuss ethical decisions involved in data reporting.

The work of the fourth- and fifth-grade students shows interesting parallels to the published reports in the media. Like the Pfizer study above, Jeremy's exploration highlighted how categories can be aggregated to hide less desirable data. When he hypothetically combined adults and children into one category of "people," the negative adult votes were diluted. Pfizer's "bundling" strategy similarly hid data that damaged their marketing goals. In the airline study, mainline carriers favored disaggregating data from their regional affiliates, while the fifth graders' argument for a sandwich/soup/salad option would have been stronger if the third-grade data were not aggregated with data from the other grades. In the lunch study the girls were aware that they were making assumptions that may have been unfounded about the third graders' experience, and that their alternative graph might unfairly silence this group.

As children gain more opportunities to gather data, and then experiment with selecting portions of it to argue different sides of an issue, the more they realize that these alternatives shape the data to fit various purposes. In turn, children can cast a more skeptical eye over the data reported by others. As critics, they can learn to question whether the data that are reported are part of a larger pool of information, and to ask who benefits from, and who is silenced by, the chosen form of presentation.

Using Direct Experience to Critique a Published Scientific Survey

In this chapter we have highlighted the relationship between children's knowledge about a survey's topic and their ability to raise questions about how data are defined, categorized, and reported. It is especially valuable when children can apply these attitudes to data texts designed by those outside of the school. The following story shows how fourth graders drew upon their extensive experience observing and documenting bird activity to critique the nature of categories in a survey designed by a highly authoritative source, the Cornell Laboratory of Ornithology.

One aspect of this study of birds was the children's participation in Project FeederWatch, operated by the Cornell Laboratory of Ornithology (see http://www.birds.cornell.edu/). Project FeederWatch is the largest scientific study of its kind that relies on data provided largely by amateurs. Scientists use the data to track broad movements of winter bird populations and long-term trends in bird distribution and abundance. They rely on the data to issue reports that impact upon environmental awareness and policy. Although the Cornell observations did not officially start until November, the fourth graders whose story is related here began observing birds at the classroom feeders as soon as the school year began (Whitin, D. J. & Whitin, P., 1998). Initially, only a few children could identify the species of any bird, but within a few weeks all of them recognized the four or five most frequent feeder visitors. They documented their observations with sketches and written notes that were regularly shared with the class. By November the children had become keen observers of the surrounding habitat, which consisted of a wooded area across an access driveway. They knew that not all came to the feeders, such as those that ate insects or the fruit on the dogwood and persimmon trees. We were confident that they were well equipped to participate responsibly in the Cornell project. Throughout the data-collecting period, students took turns staffing the window and making reports to the class. Their long-term involvement with the Project gave them an insider's view of the work of ornithologists. At the conclusion of the study, they drew upon this knowledge to raise critical questions about the Laboratory's end-of-study report.

The report form included a bubble-in questionnaire that called for information about the particular habitat of the observation area. One section asked for estimates of the number of several kinds of trees:

- Evergreen trees less than 3m tall
- Evergreen shrubs (or saplings) 3m tall or less
- Deciduous trees greater than 3m tall
- Deciduous shrubs (or saplings) less than 3m tall
- Fruiting trees or shrubs

After a trip outside to tabulate this information, the children expressed dissatisfaction with these specified categories. One problem centered on fruiting trees. Dogwoods and persimmons bear fruit, but they lose their leaves. Should the trees be included in both the "fruiting tree" and "deciduous" categories? If so, would Cornell have an accurate portrayal of their habitat? The children were very serious about this question because the fruit trees, particularly the persimmon, had attracted some species (e.g., the yellow-bellied sapsucker) that were seen only in that context. In their view, the lack of clarity on the form could contribute to misinformation in the data report.

The children also felt that Cornell had omitted an important category of trees. The wooded area near the feeders included several dead trees, but the form did not include this category as an option. The children knew that allowing dead trees to remain in a habitat was an environmentally sound practice for many bird species. Woodpeckers collect insects from these trees, and they, as well as several other cavity-nesting species, make their homes there. The children insisted that "dead trees" was an essential category. Fortunately, the form included space for comments, and they confidently included their recommendations in their report.

This experience benefited the children in several ways. The questions they raised demonstrated that how data are categorized determines what information is revealed and concealed. Most importantly, the children were not passive participants who deferred decision-making authority to an institution of power. They were able to raise critical questions about the Cornell survey because they had knowledge of both the subject matter and the data-gathering process, and they took action by making recommendations for the revisions to the categories. They also gained insight into the Laboratory as authors. As writers themselves, they realized that authors consider their audience. As they discussed the Cornell survey, they realized that the authors of the survey faced a similar situation. They reasoned that the Laboratory probably wanted to make the instrument simple, and so it chose to include categories of vegetation that were most typical to participants. It is likely that most Project participants did not have dead trees in their habitats. As authors, the Cornell staff had to make compromises to accommodate their audience. In raising these issues, the fourth graders better understood that despite the level of authority of the authors, all data-collection instruments have limitations. The children gained appreciation for the fact that all data texts, including scientific surveys, are human constructs that can be examined and critiqued. Their experience underscores once again the value of giving children opportunities to use their own areas of knowledge and expertise as a bridge to critique data texts in the public arena.

Next Steps: Strategies for Critiquing Definitions and Categories

The stories in this chapter show that the interpretation of statistical texts depends heavily on the definitions and categories of data. Some strategies for incorporating these critical dimensions include the following:

- *How might teachers capitalize on children's personal and experiential knowledge to support them in interrogating their own definitions and categories?*
- *How might vocabulary studies be expanded to include the socio-cultural or political implications of choosing definitions?*
- *How might role-playing help children imagine the perspectives of various groups impacted by a data report?*
- *How can teachers capitalize upon unexpected responses in children's data-gathering experiences to underscore the complexities of creating categories?*
- *How can teachers support children to grapple with the tension between simplifying categories of data for clarity and providing sufficient details for accuracy and equity?*
- *In what ways can children select and/or recombine different portions of a large dataset and examine how those alternatives promote particular points of view? What groups of people might benefit from each scenario? What groups of people might be silenced or marginalized?*
- *How can children use their personal expertise and experience as a bridge to critique published data reports, survey instruments, and rankings?*

4
Creating the Visual
Playing Statistical Hide and Seek

> The greatest value of a picture is when it forces us to notice what we never expected to see.
>
> John Tukey (Tukey, 1997, p. vi)

In one first-grade class individual children took turns surveying their class-mates about topics of interest (Whitin, 1997). On these occasions the teacher gave the children blank paper so that they could take charge of recording the information in a way that made sense to them. One child decided to ask her classmates, "Do you have a pet?" Figure 4.1 shows the results of her poll. She chose to draw profiles of dogs and cats to record the responses. When some answers involved two pets, she placed the corresponding profiles close together, while single pet owners were noted by only one of the appropriate figures. In choosing to represent her data in this way, she captured three layers of information, i.e., the number of pets owned by the class members (14), the number of pet owners (10), and the number of multiple pet owners (4).

As a contrast, the teacher challenged the girl to show the same information in another way. This time she organized the data by the type of pet, which she placed in separate, horizontal rows (Figure 4.2). During class meeting time, both visuals were shared. One classmate commented that he liked the "double drawings" on the first visual because "you can see who has more than one animal to feed." In comparing the two displays, the children noted that the organized rows of pets made it easier to count and compare the totals of each kind of pet (e.g., more dogs than cats). However, by displaying the data in this way this young author did not show two of the layers of information, namely double ownership and the total number of owners.

The first-grade children in this class were learning key ideas about visual representations that underlie a critical orientation toward data. Their analysis of the "double drawings" was a first step in building an understanding of the particular affordances of visual information. For instance, the "double drawing" pet visual efficiently condensed a lot of information in an efficient manner. Visuals are particularly valuable in highlighting relationships, since the reader/viewer sees everything simultaneously and as a whole (Kress, 2000). In this case the children could quickly see how many people owned multiple pets, and what kinds of pets belonged to each person. Imagining what the same information might look like in written form highlights the different way in which each form of communication works. A narrative about pets might read,

Figure 4.1 Child's representation for the survey question, "Do you have a pet?" Whitin, D. J. (1997, January). Collecting data with young children. *Young Children*, 52(2), 28–32. Copyright by author.

"Brigette has a dog and a cat. Joshua has one dog. Michael has two dogs. . . ." Since the information is presented in a sequential manner, each fact seems separate from the others, and therefore it is difficult to summarize the data. Further, the relationships among owners are more cumbersome to notice than they were in the visual format.

The teacher's decision to ask the child to represent the data in another way sowed the seeds of two other important ideas about data-related visuals. First, the girl and her classmates were beginning to discover that authors have choices. Second, as the children actively analyzed what was lost and what was gained by representing the data in organized rows, they were building an

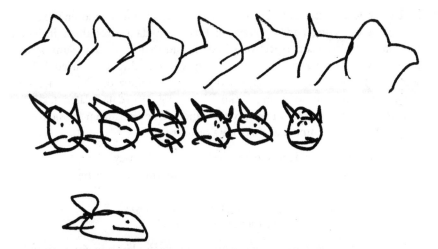

Figure 4.2 Alternative representation for the same "pet" data. Whitin, D. J. (1997, January). Collecting data with young children. *Young Children*, 52(2), 28–32. Copyright by author.

understanding that all visual representations reveal some relationships and conceal others. Such a realization underscores the notion that having choices enables authors to show information in particular ways to tell particular stories. Visual texts, as any other form of communication, are not neutral, but instead reflect the authors' interests, values, motives, and beliefs (Gee, 1992; Kress, 2000). Even in a visual text as simple as the double silhouette pet graph, the form reflects the child's interest in capturing ownership of multiple pets. As children become familiar with exploring the design choices that authors make and their effects, they build an understanding that authors can create visual representations that position the reader/viewer to notice certain relationships and not others (Janks, 2010).

With these points in mind, it follows that a critical orientation toward data must include attention to the specialized kind of visual literacy involved in composing graphs and other statistical displays. From a critic's perspective, it is therefore important for children to be knowledgeable about the potentials and limitations of various data displays, both conventional formats such as pie charts and line graphs, as well as visuals of their own design. They need to explore and analyze the way in which authors use visual elements such as shape, size, and spatial relationships to guide the viewer's attention (Tufte, 1983). They benefit from many experiences using and evaluating the appropriateness of different kinds of graphs for a wide range of purposes (Williams & Joseph, 1993). They widen their perspectives by imagining how alternative ways to display the same data might tell a different story.

The strategies described here are rooted in the belief that children's experience with collecting and representing their own data gives them insights that nurture a critic's perspective. Children find that in order to summarize the results, some finer grained information is almost always sacrificed. When some relationships are highlighted, others are minimized. This awareness is an important part of being a skillful composer of data-related texts as well as an informed critic of the texts of others. Questions from the heuristic (Figure 1.2) can prompt analysis of data displays:

- Why did you decide to show the information this way?
- What information is concealed/revealed by this form of representation?
- Who benefits from representing the data in this way?
- How else could you have displayed your data?

To illustrate these ideas we show a range of different kinds of visual displays of information, including conventional bar graphs and pie charts, invented representations, and data maps. In these examples we highlight how children explore choices while constructing graphs, and how they are encouraged to analyze these representations from a critical perspective. The opening two stories describe children examining different layers of information, from favorite characters from *The Wizard of Oz*, to a survey on family chores and getting a weekly allowance. The following two stories highlight further choices authors have in representing statistical information: deciding whether a bar graph or a pie chart best emphasizes the main point an author is trying to make (about problems with food preparation at school); and examining how different scales on a line graph suggest contrasting conclusions. Finally, the last two stories show how authors can use data maps to depict spatial relationships that are not possible with other graphical kinds of representation (the proximity of churches to restaurants, and the location of homes in a neighborhood). We also share how professionals use data maps to document important relationships: the link between student obesity and the proximity of fast food restaurants and schools; and a depiction of the foreclosure crisis in New York City that exposed the long history of financial discrimination against minority populations. In all these examples we underscore how authors have choices about how they represent their data. They select a form of representation that they consider to be the best for conveying what they want to say (Jewitt & Kress, 2003). Therefore, critics need to ask questions about those choices and interrogate those decisions.

Comparing and Contrasting Visual Displays with Young Children

As the example of pet ownership shows, the comparing and contrasting of different displays of data can help to highlight how authors of statistical texts have choices about how to represent that information. By analyzing these choices children can learn to examine data with a critic's eye. Similarly, in

Chapter 1 the kindergarten children critiqued the original class apple graph because it didn't show their preferences for sliced or unsliced fruit. By revising the data display, these layers of information were revealed. We will now look at another example from an early childhood classroom in which children graphed data related to a favorite piece of children's literature.

The children in a kindergarten class represented a set of data using two different representations: towers of snap cubes as well as a pictograph (Whitin, P. & Whitin, D.J., 2003). They were able to see how each representation afforded them certain potentials and limitations. The investigation began when the children were cast as Munchkins in the fifth-grade production of *The Wizard of Oz*. The children's excitement for the story grew when Phyllis read aloud the novel, and they began to imagine themselves cast as various major characters. Phyllis decided to involve the children in constructing a class graph to represent these role-playing choices, and to incorporate two data representations familiar to the children during the process. The children had routinely tallied the daily hot–cold lunch count with two colors of snap cubes, and they also had previous experience with simple pictographs showing data related to such topics as birthdays and lost teeth.

Snap cubes can be used as an efficient tool to make a quick but tangible tally. In this case, Phyllis assembled seven baskets of different colored cubes, one color for each of the major characters. During center time, children took turns selecting an appropriate cube and placing it on a card next to the basket. As the various towers grew (or stayed small), the children made spontaneous comments (e.g., "Dorothy has a lot!" or "Two people voted for Oz"). This hands-on material, easily combined as "bars," contributed to their active involvement in interpretation. On the other hand, the identity of who cast what vote was lost (Figure 4.3).

The class constructed the pictograph on the following day. First, each child selected a paper square that corresponded to the color of the cube (or character) that they had previously selected. We instructed the children to draw the character and to write down the reason why this one was their favorite (Figure 4.4). The completed graph thus incorporated several layers of information: how many children chose each character, which child cast what vote, and the reason for the choice (Figure 4.5). For instance, there were several reasons for choosing Dorothy, including: "She is smart," and "I like it when Dorothy slapped the lion on the nose." When the class assembled to interpret the pictograph, they made numerical comparisons (e.g., "There are 10 Dorothys but only two Totos") as well as comments about the written information (e.g., "Me and Cameron, we did the Oz. Cameron said we were the faker dudes because he fakes them. He wanted to be the Wizard of Oz"). Thus, these reasons for selecting a particular character, as well as the identification of which student chose which of these characters, were layers of information that were *not* conveyed by the snap cube representation.

Figure 4.3 Snap-cube graph representing responses to the question, "What Oz character would you like to be?" Whitin, P. & Whitin, D.J. (2003). Developing mathematical understanding along the Yellow Brick Road. *Young Children*, 58(1), 36–40. Copyright by author.

As the discussion continued, David used one child's observation to highlight another difference between these two visual representations. When observing the pictograph, Michele noticed that several characters had two votes. She pointed to each column of twos as she counted a total of 10 children. Even though Michele was able to indicate how high this imagined stack of two-votes would be, the pieces of paper remained fixed in place. The paper graph, despite its rich layers of information, was limited in this way. We surmised that many of the other children were not able to mentally add several columns together as Michele had done on this paper graph. Since the cubes could be physically manipulated, we thought that using this material would make the idea of combining the columns accessible to all the children. We posed this invitation: "Michele was imagining that she was moving each group of two and putting them together to make a column of 10. But if we used the cubes on our other graph we could actually move those sets of two and really put them on top of each other. I wonder what other ways we could combine those columns of cubes."

We provided the children with this opportunity during center time. As they re-enacted some of these numerical relationships the advantages of this concrete material became evident to them in a new way. They combined and recombined different columns to show various sums. For example, the children physically took the five sets of 2s that represented the groups of two votes each, snapped them together, and then matched it directly to the combined bar of

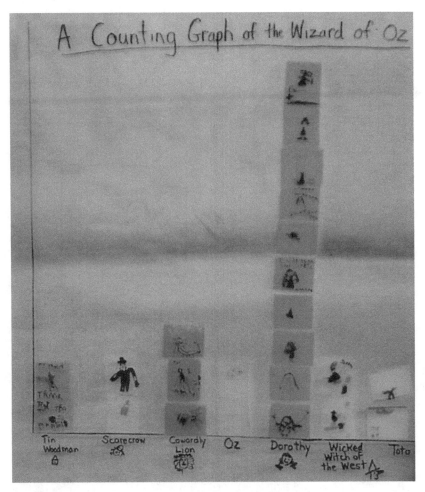

Figure 4.4 Pictograph of favorite Oz characters Whitin, P. & Whitin, D.J. (2003). Developing mathematical understanding along the Yellow Brick Road. *Young Children*, 58(1), 36–40. Copyright by author.

10 cubes next to the tower of 10 Dorothy votes. The children also made new discoveries that extended the pictograph discussion. For instance, Michele added four cubes to the 10 orange "Dorothys," and explained, "Before we put these on we had four. But now we have 14." Then, breaking off the 10, she continued, "If you broke this [10], you would have four." In this way she acted out the inverse relationship between addition and subtraction. Revisiting the snap cubes provided an additional opportunity to discuss with the children the potentials of each form of representation.

In summary, these stories of the pet and Oz graphs show that even young children can build an understanding of how different forms of representation

Figure 4.5 Children's individual representations of the reasons for selecting their favorite Oz character. A. "I like how she melted." B. "He growls all of the time." C. "Oz: Faker Dudes" D. "She is smart." E. "I like when Dorothy slapped the lion on the nose."

can highlight different relationships, and that authors make choices that reflect their interests and points of view. In the following three stories we discuss other ways in which authors can visually manipulate data to serve a particular purpose. The first story shows how false relationships can be implied when two pieces of data are displayed together. The second describes children debating whether a bar graph or a pie chart would be better in persuading their audience of the need to make changes in the school's cafeteria service, and the third involves the issue of scale.

Exposing Misrepresented Relationships in Multi-layered Graphs

Sometimes graphs can show some misleading relationships. This issue was raised unexpectedly when two fifth-grade boys, Richard and Shaun, collected some information about chores that children did at home. (Two of their classmates collected the data described in Chapter 1.) The two boys polled their classmates by asking: "Do you have chores to do at home? Do you ever try to get out of chores, and how do you do that? Do you get paid for chores?" They first decided to graph the responses to "getting out of chores," which they labeled "excuses." Although nine children said they did not try to avoid chores, there were others who cited specific excuses. The boys grouped the responses into the following categories: "Sleep" (e.g., "I try to act like I am sleeping"), "Act Like Reading" (e.g., "I just get a book and try to study"), "Sibling" (e.g., "I tell my brother he's lazy and he should do it"), "Hide" (e.g., "I go somewhere so my parents can't find me"), "Ask Double" (e.g., "I ask for a double raise in my pay"), "Forget" (e.g., "Sometimes I just forget"). Next they each constructed a graph.

As they were working, David challenged the children to add a second layer of information to their graphs that combined the data on excuses with the data on who gets paid for doing chores. David knew that constructing graphs with multiple layers of information is an important visual strategy, and was eager to see how the children might accomplish this task. Richard decided to create a series of symbols on his graph to show these data: $ represented getting paid, and other symbols reinforced the particular category of excuse, such as Z for sleep, a door for hiding, a stick figure for sibling, and so on. The squares above each excuse were either divided in half, one part representing the icon for the excuse, and the other part representing a dollar sign; or there was just an icon for the excuse and no dollar sign (see examples in Figure 4.6).

Although this visual display did indeed combine these two layers of information, it also set up a misleading relationship. This problem became apparent when David asked Richard to create a title for his graph. Both boys brainstormed several ideas, but none seemed appropriate: "Chores and Cash," but they realized the graph is really about excuses; "Excuses for Chores and Cash," but the graph is not about excuses for cash; "Excuses for Chores and

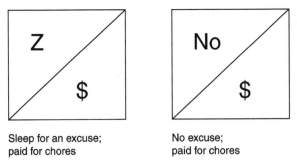

Sleep for an excuse;   No excuse;
paid for chores   paid for chores

Figure 4.6 Symbols representing excuses for chores and getting paid for chores.

Still Got Cash," but some children did *not* use excuses and still got paid. Richard finally concluded that perhaps he should not even put in the "cash part" because it didn't seem to fit. He therefore decided upon "Excuses for Chores," followed by a string of dollar signs (Figure 4.7). This compromise made it apparent that the graph lacked a main point or focus. In the context of this discussion the implied relationship between chores and getting paid was questioned. As the children and David analyzed this relationship further they realized that Richard's visual was conveying a misleading relationship (e.g., that children who give an excuse for chores still get paid). For instance, the results of the graph show that three people used "sleep" as an excuse and these same three people were also paid for doing chores. However, the boys realized that they could *not* conclude, "Three kids get paid for chores when they pretend to sleep." It is likely that these children did do their chores on other occasions. Through this experience, the children and David all learned a valuable lesson: combining data from two different questions into a single visual can sometimes convey a false and misleading relationship. Originally, Richard and Shaun had thought of constructing a separate bar graph on who was paid for chores and who was not. In hindsight this decision would have been the better choice.

It is also interesting to note that this struggle to find the appropriate words for the title caused us to look more closely at the mathematics. Creating statistical texts is a multimodal venture in which each representational form informs the others. In addition, David's willingness to admit to the children that he was the instigator of this misleading—but unanticipated—representation helped support this disposition for critiquing. By taking risks to display data in different ways, learners gain insiders' understanding of the potentials and limitations of statistical representations.

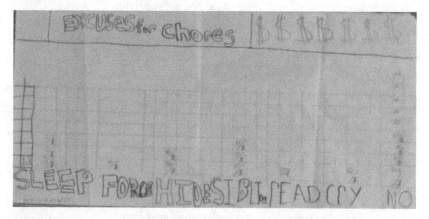

Figure 4.7 "Excuses for Chores" graph that also includes data about being paid for chores.

Matching Graphical Form to Purpose

The fifth-grade children involved in the lunch program survey described in Chapters 2 and 3 were busy summarizing their data for the report to the principal and school board. Part of their data concerned issues revolving around food preparation. Initial survey data had identified that the most commonly expressed complaints were that food sometimes was not hot, that it was undercooked, or that it was soggy. In a follow-up survey they had posed the question, "If you aren't happy with something for lunch, what is usually the reason?" To respond, participants could circle one or two of these choices. Of the 90 responses, "too soggy" totaled 29; "not hot enough," 24, and "not cooked enough," 37.

What kind of graph would be most effective to represent these results? Like authors of any genre, Brittaney and Keaton, the children responsible for this portion of the report, needed to consider the main point that they wanted the audience to recognize. Together with Phyllis, they entered the data on an Excel worksheet and displayed the results as a bar graph, the format with which they had the most experience (Figure 4.8). They kept this document open and made a second version, this time as a pie chart (Figure 4.9).

Initially, Brittaney favored the bar graph, suggesting that the principal would want to "know all the numbers." It was disconcerting to her that the raw numbers of 29, 24, and 37 on the pie chart responses changed to "different numbers", i.e. 32%, 27%, and 41%. Using numbers that seemed once-removed

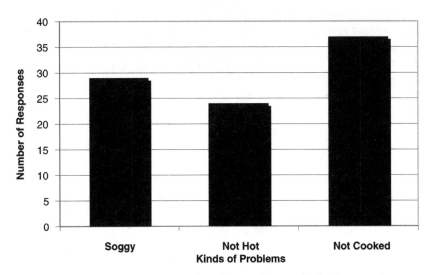

Figure 4.8 Bar graph showing survey data about problems with food preparation.

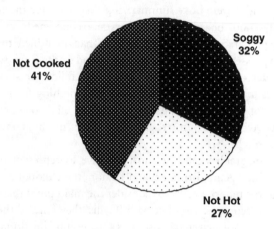

Problems with Food

Figure 4.9 Pie chart showing the same survey data about food preparation.

from the discrete data bothered her because percentages didn't seem like the "real numbers." This was important assessment information. From her comments, it was apparent that she did not have a firm understanding of what percentages are and how they are obtained, since the software program had done the calculations for her. We therefore spent some time reviewing percentages as a ratio and illustrating the concept using the familiar context of classroom test grades. This aspect of the experience highlighted for us that a firm understanding of mathematical concepts is an essential part of being an informed, flexible author of statistical texts.

After this review, we again considered the "food preparation" pie chart. Keaton argued that this form was the better representation: "This one has more of an impact because it gives it out of 100; it gives percentages. Like 'not cooked' is 41%. That's close to 50% and the pie chart shows that. But you can't see how it's close to one half on the bar graph. It's harder to see." By using the benchmark of ½ as a point of comparison Keaton was noting how the parts relate to a whole in a pie chart. Phyllis agreed, adding, "As a viewer, when I see the pie chart, I see that 'soggy' is a bit larger as you said, but I also see that all three are quite big. There is no part that's just a tiny slice." Since the children wanted to emphasize that all three concerns were prominent ones that deserved equal attention from the principal, they therefore chose to use the pie chart to display their information. Through this experience, they were learning that one of their roles as composers of data displays is to guide the viewer to see what relationships are most important (Tufte, 1983). At the same time, they were aware that they made their choice based upon their intentions and interests (Kress, 2003; Janks, 2010).

Using Different Scales to Tell Different Stories

Another choice that authors of data-related texts have involves which scale to use in the construction of line graphs. This issue arose when we shared *Tiger Math* (Nagda & Bickel, 2000) with a second group of fifth-grade students. It is the true story of a Siberian tiger named TJ who was born in the Denver Zoo. When he was 10 weeks old his mother died and TJ then refused to eat. The veterinarians decided to force feed him in order to keep him alive. After some tense moments TJ finally began to eat and grew to be a healthy tiger. The story is told through words as well as graphs. There is a graph on each two-page spread to tell more of TJ's story. There are bar graphs, line graphs, and pie charts to show TJ's weight, his food consumption, and the number of tigers in the wild. After reading and discussing the story we invited the children to choose one graph from the story and re-represent the same data with another kind of graph. In this way the children could develop a critic's perspective by comparing the two representations to see how certain relationships become revealed and concealed in each one. One pair of students wanted to use a line graph to show the same information that was shown on a bar graph in the book. The graph represented the amount of ounces of meat that TJ ate over the course of six weeks. Before the children began to work on their own individual graphs David took this opportunity to explore how authors can use scale in line graphs to tell quite different stories. He used two widely different scales (the unit of ½ and the unit of 10) to graph this data on TJ's meat consumption in order to exaggerate the effect. David drew both line graphs on the whiteboard and then asked the children to compare these two new graphs (Figures 4.10 and 4.11). He emphasized again that both of these line graphs showed the same data but were constructed with different scales.

After some discussion Byron noted the inverse relationship between the size of the unit and the amount the line will rise: "I noticed that the more value the numbers have on a scale, the less the numbers will go up. I also noticed that the less value the numbers have on a scale, the more the line will go up." Louis observed, "The line [on the unit of 10 scale graph] doesn't shoot all the way up like on the other graph." Using Lance's words as an example we discussed with the children how the size of the measuring unit on a scale impacts on the kind of language we can use to describe the data. The ½-unit scale affords us the opportunity to use words such as "shoots up," "increases a lot," and "rises rapidly." whereas the 10-unit scale frames our language choices with different words, such as "goes up a little bit," "doesn't change too much," and "stays steady." In this way the words and the visual are intertwined to create a more powerful argument, positioning readers to view the world in a particular way.

David then asked the children to consider how each line graph might impact on the telling of TJ's story. We discussed how these data were presented at a

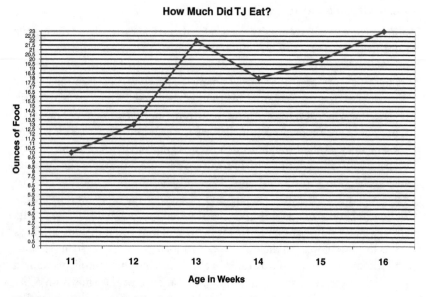

Figure 4.10 Line graph of the baby tiger's meat consumption shown with a scale of one-half.

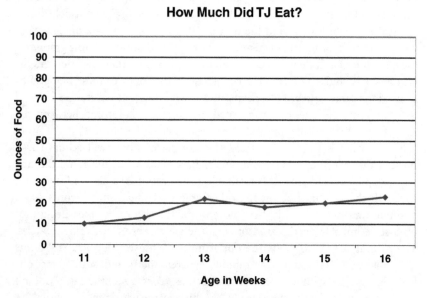

Figure 4.11 Line graph of the baby tiger's food intake shown with a scale of 10.

critical point in the story. TJ had not been eating and he was admitted to the hospital so that the veterinarians could force feed him to try to increase his weight. After a few weeks he did begin to eat on his own and his weight slowly increased. Depending upon the scale used one could tell a tale of TJ's appetite either improving dramatically or modestly. Creating these different scales in the context of a story that the children cared about helped to accentuate the contrasting outcomes that could have been told.

The example of these two different scales helped to show how authors can manipulate scale for effect (e.g., to minimize or maximize a trend, problem, or issue). Scale affects the stories we tell and impacts on the language we use to craft those stories. From a critical perspective scale becomes a tool for framing the world as authors would like others to see it. And seeing becomes believing unless children learn to raise such critical questions as "Why was this scale used? To what effect? What if another scale had been used?" As we have emphasized throughout this book, critics need to develop a habit of mind that says, "Things could be otherwise." This "otherwiseness" is an essential perspective for viewing data-related texts.

Data Maps: Describing Data in a Spatial Context

So far we have discussed the ways in which different visual representations can conceal and reveal a variety of relationships. Data maps are a specialized visual form that show a spatial context of numerical information. Although this representational form emerged in the seventeenth century, it became widely recognized in 1854 owing to the now classic work of Dr. John Snow, who pioneered one of the earliest applications of mapping in medical investigations. The city of London was in crisis, severely affected by a cholera epidemic. Although careful records were kept about the number of deaths and where they were occurring, finding a cause eluded physicians until Dr. Snow plotted the data on a street map (Figure 4.12). The locations of victims' homes formed clusters around certain public water pumps, while few deaths were recorded near others. Given this information, the affected pumps were then closed down, and the epidemic, now clearly related to contaminated water, subsided.

Since that groundbreaking discovery, data maps have played an important role in medicine as well as in other fields. Today epidemiologists use data maps to investigate possible links between environmental factors and diseases, such as asthma and cancer. Politicians use maps to examine the distribution of voter preferences, meteorologists plot drought conditions, and so on. Thus, data maps have the unique potential to show spatial and numerical relationships, and therefore deserve attention in elementary classrooms. In the following sections we show ways in which children used mapping to display information, as well as the ways in which they exposed the limitations of their work. We parallel their investigations to examples from the professional world.

Yards
50 0 50 100 150 200
x Pump •Deaths from cholera

Figure 4.12 Dr. John Snow's historic data map of a London neighborhood that established the connection between polluted water and the 1854 cholera epidemic. Water pumps are designated by "x" and cholera deaths by dots. The pump near the "d" in "Broad Street" was linked to the highest concentration of deaths. Public domain.

Data Maps Give Perspectives on Marketing Issues

Marc and Bryson, two seventh graders, passed a McDonald's while riding their bikes to Burger King one Sunday afternoon. They noticed that McDonald's was crowded while Burger King was practically empty. They recalled this experience when they were assigned a project as part of a unit of a study of consumerism and marketing in their language arts class (Freppon, 2001). The project requirements included collecting, interpreting, and presenting data relevant to their topic, supported with visual and written artifacts. It was the students' responsibility to choose a form of visual that best matched the information and purpose of their study. The students developed a wide range of topics to study (e.g., product safety, kinds of advertising and other marketing strategies, and guarantees). For some of the students, pie charts, bar graphs, and tables were the most appropriate visual forms to report their data. As Marc and Bryson developed their project, a map proved to be the best choice for reasons similar to Dr. Snow's.

Thinking back on their experience with McDonald's and Burger King, the boys wondered why some restaurants had a higher volume of customers than others. Both boys' families regularly ate out at family-style restaurants after Sunday church services. They therefore hypothesized that restaurants close to churches might have the highest customer volume. They decided to canvass area restaurants and obtain information about the number of patrons between 12 noon and 2 p.m. on Sundays.

In tabulating their data, they sorted the restaurants into three groups: fast food, sit-down dining, and take-out. They used color-coded stickers to designate churches as well as the types of restaurants, and plotted the locations of each on a hand-drawn map (Figure 4.13). They had rejected the idea of using a commercial town map because they thought it would have too many unnecessary details, and therefore would distract the viewer. Their decision showed their consideration for the audience. Finally, they added the customer volume for each restaurant in a legend. Their accompanying narrative read:

> On this poster we have marked the location of churches in relation to three types of food facilities: Dining rooms, fast food, and take-out restaurants. Our study showed that more people went out to eat at sit-down dining facilities between 12:00 and 2:00 on Sunday than ate at fast food restaurants or took home prepared food from take-out restaurants.

The legend notes that take-out restaurants drew 10–50 customers, while fast food attracted between 60 and 300, and "dining-room" facilities had crowds of 300–1,000. The map, however, reveals information and relationships that are

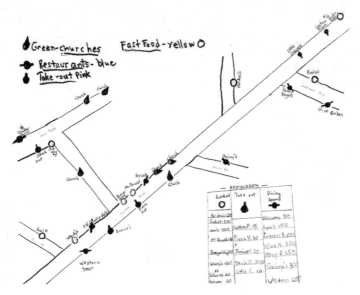

Figure 4.13 Data map of restaurants and churches.

concealed by the list form. The map shows two clusters of churches. The two restaurants with the highest customer volume were each located near a church cluster. In contrast, the two dining-room restaurants with the fewest patrons were both on a side road some distance from either cluster of churches. Thus, information from the data map gave the boys evidence to distinguish between restaurants within a category (dining-room facilities), in a similar way to how Dr. Snow differentiated between contaminated and clean water pumps. In Bryson's words, "You can see on the paper [legend and written narrative] how many people they got. You don't really see how close [the restaurants] are to the church or anything, but when you label the stickers and everything [on the map], you can see the churches, and the restaurants by the churches, and see all the ones way far away don't get hardly any people."

An option that the boys didn't pursue was visually representing the customer volume on the map in addition to giving the numerical information in the legend. For example, they could have varied the proportionate size of the dots to add this layer of information. Examining examples from the media might have given them alternative ideas for their map.

After the boys presented their project to the class, their teacher wanted them to further consider the motives that could lie behind publicizing data of this nature. She asked the boys who would find the data useful. Bryson answered, "Probably people who want to start a business. They might want to build it by a church to get a lot more business." However, the boys also realized the limitations of their study. They wondered what kind of business the various restaurants did during the week and on Saturdays. In fact, they reasoned, other restaurants might get "a whole bunch more business" during the week. Take-out restaurants, for example, had low customer volume on Sunday, but, as Bryson noted, "I don't know anybody who would go home and call out Pizza Hut after church." However, pizza would be a likely choice "on a Friday night or during the week when you're real tired, or after work, or something." Thus, their data map told only part of the story. In fact, people starting a business could be misled if they only saw these data related to Sunday lunch times. The boys were learning that even data maps have both potentials and limitations, and that these visual forms also reflect the interests of their authors.

These seventh graders suggested that the use of maps might be a helpful tool for people starting a business. Similarly, epidemiologists have found mapping to be useful in studying health problems. A recent investigation of business location and community health incorporated both of these factors. Economists at the University of California and Columbia University used maps to show a link between student obesity and the proximity of fast-food restaurants to schools (Rabin, 2009). The researchers studied millions of schoolchildren and found that ninth graders who attended a school which was within one-tenth of a mile of a fast-food restaurant were more likely to be obese than students whose schools were a quarter of a mile or further away.

Although this study suggests a causal relationship between these two factors, namely geographic proximity to these restaurants and obesity, the researchers noted limitations to their conclusions. They admitted that they did not know *why* students were affected in this way. The researchers realized that there were probably several reasons why students might have patronized these fast-food restaurants. Some of these possible, but undocumented explanations, included: "It could be that the students don't like to wander too far. Maybe they don't have a long lunch period. Maybe it's just the effect of having temptation right in front of your eyes" (p.A16). Thus, the researchers, like the children, used maps to investigate a relationship, and were also cognizant of the limitations of their findings.

Using Data Maps to Describe Neighborhoods

A group of first-grade children also experimented with representing data spatially. Their teacher had overheard several of her children discussing some new trailer homes in the area. One child in particular was sharing with his friends all the new features in this trailer. Soon the children were telling each other about what kind of structure they lived in. Since this topic was of such special interest to several of the children, the teacher invited two of them, Cory and Sam, to survey their friends about their homes. The surveyors decided to ask their friends if they lived in a trailer, house, or apartment. For logistical reasons the teacher asked each child to poll half the class and create a visual representation of their findings. As it turned out, one of the visuals included a map, and the other did not. This contrast allowed the children to view the benefits of spatially representing the same data in different ways.

As the children set out on their task they sometimes received more information than they had first requested: "I live in the white brick house"; "My house is the last house on that dirt road"; "We have a double-wide trailer"; "I live at grandma's house." These details inspired Sam to develop a map to record some of this information in his visual.

Once they were finished they shared their findings with the class. Cory was the first person to share his results (Figure 4.14). He reported: "Three children live in houses, six children live in trailers, and no one lives in an apartment." He wrote a "T" or an "H" beside his drawings to designate either "trailer" or "house." He grouped his responses together into those two categories. He also decided to write the names of two students who came to class late and whom he had not yet interviewed. He wrote his final tabulations at the bottom of his paper: 6 t, 3 h, 0 p (6 trailers, 3 houses, 0 apartments). Thus, his visual contained several layers of information: names of occupants; type of housing; and students not yet interviewed.

When Sam shared his data about the other half of the class's homes, it became clear that his visual contained some additional layers of information (Figure 4.15). He explained: "Five kids live in trailers, six live in houses and no

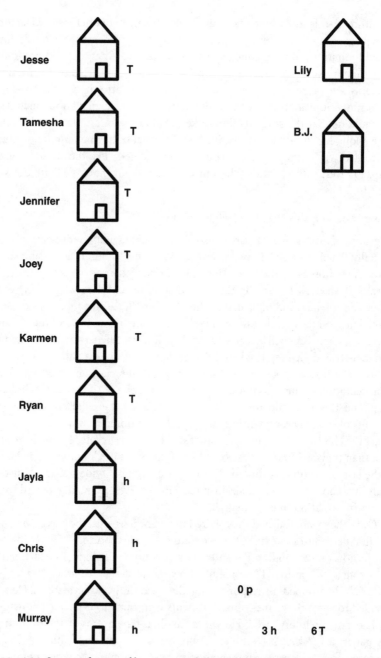

Figure 4.14 Survey of types of homes recorded in list format. "T" stands for "trailer," "H" for "house," and "P" for "apartment." Facsimile of original.

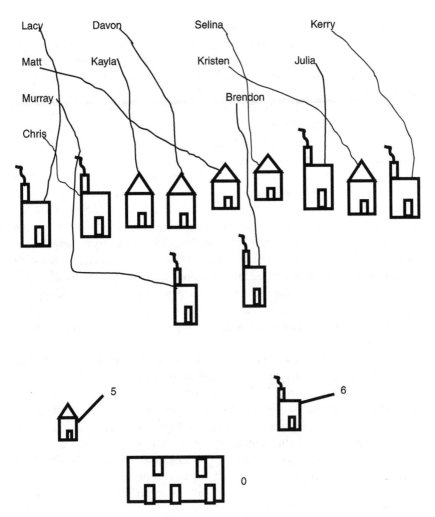

Figure 4.15 Data map of types of homes. Facsimile of original.

one lives in an apartment." He had drawn chimneys on some of the structures to distinguish houses from trailers. However, because he had drawn a map he was able to show spatial relations as well. He described these additional details as he pointed to his map and told the class: "Davon, Kayla, Matt and Selina live next door to each other in trailers. Murray lives in a house across the street from them. Lacy lives in a big brick house. And Kerry lives in a house down at the end of the road." Since the children had the freedom to represent their data in their own way they were able to demonstrate to the class different ways in which similar data could be shown.

The teacher wanted to highlight even further this issue of the decisions people make in choosing what to visually represent. So she asked them if there was any other information they had learned from their classmates that they chose not to depict on their visual. They listed several other pieces of data that were not shown: "We could have colored the houses to show what colors they really are; and we could have shown who has green grass and who has no grass at all; and we could have shown who lives in a double-wide trailer, and who lives in a new trailer." Here again, the children were learning that their visual only represented part of the data that they collected. This story helps to show that even young children can create and critique data maps to depict spatial relationships when the topic is tied to their interests and experiences.

Just as these children used maps to represent several layers of information about their neighborhood, so did Damon Rich, an urban designer and waterfront planner. He was commissioned to transform the 9,335-square-foot Panorama of the City of New York, an architectural model built for the 1964 World's Fair, into a representation that showed the "sprawling nature of the foreclosure crisis in New York City" (Cohen, 2009, p. C1). Along with a team of student assistants he affixed a pink triangle to any block on this three-dimensional map where there were three or more foreclosures. Once this map was completed it showed clusters of pink triangles that enabled visitors to see "in a single glance precisely where the subprime lenders wreaked the most havoc" (p. C1).

This additional layer of information about foreclosures highlighted what some have called "reverse redlining." Redlining was a practice that was rampant in the city in the 1970s in which minorities (primarily African-American and Latino) were systemically denied mortgage loans. This transformed exhibit showed that these same minorities were now being discriminated against in a "reverse way" through being targeted by unscrupulous lenders who convinced them to assume loans they would never be able to repay. Thus, the pink flags that were added to this urban panorama helped to represent the long history of "predatory and racist lending practices" in New York City (p. C7). Thus, both this urban designer and the first-grade student capitalized on the spatial potential of mapping to efficiently and succinctly express a range of relationships.

Next Steps: Strategies for Critiquing Visual Information

The stories in this chapter suggest some possible questions for promoting this critical perspective toward visual information. Some of these include:

- *How can children represent the same set of data in two different ways? What relationships does each one reveal and conceal? Who benefits from having the data displayed in this way rather than the other way?*
- *How can children be encouraged to invent their own visual representation for their data?*
- *How can children be supported to include several layers of information into a single visual? How does this multi-layered approach serve the*

author's purpose? In what ways might the visual convey some false or misleading relationships?

- *In what ways can children create different scales for a set of data to minimize or dramatize the changes in those data? Which scale best promotes an author's point of view? Who benefits or is silenced by these variations?*
- *How can children critique the graphs they see in the media or in their textbooks? How can children use the insights they gained themselves as authors of statistical texts to pose questions about the graphs of others? Why did this author choose this form of representation to show the data? How might the information look different if it were presented in another form?*

5

What We Don't Know
Critiquing the Sample and the Conclusions

> Something is, in short, always missing. In evaluating statistics, we should not forget what is lost, if only because this helps us understand what we still have.
>
> Joel Best (Best, 2004, p. 25)

A kindergarten class had just completed a bar graph of their eye color. The teacher led them in a discussion of the data by asking them what they had noticed. They noted the number for each color and made comparisons among the colors. Then the teacher asked, "What does our graph *not* tell us? What do we *not* know when we look at our graph?" One child responded, "It doesn't tell what color eyes your mama has!" Other children then offered additional observations: "It doesn't tell what color eyes your daddy has"; "It doesn't tell what color eyes your brother has, or your sister"; "It doesn't tell if anyone in your family has the same eyes as you!"

By posing this question about what is missing, the teacher enabled the children to note the limitations of their graph. Every graph is limited because it is a product of choices. In this case the children's observations highlighted that the sample was restricted to only the children in this class. The teacher's questions helped the children see how the size of the sample influenced what they could say about their results and conclusions. Owing to the restricted sample size, the children could only report results pertaining to their class. They could not make any conclusions about the eye color of their family members.

This story highlights how any report of statistical information is only a partial accounting, a point that we have made throughout this book. During the data-gathering process some choices were made and others abandoned. So critics ask, "Why this question/definition/visual rather than another one?" Since some choices reveal certain relationships and conceal others, there are always limitations to a given set of data. In this chapter we consider limitations about the nature of the sample, the relationship between results and conclusions, and the potential benefits and drawbacks to using various mathematical concepts such as ratio and average. Guiding questions about the sample and the conclusions include the following.

The Sample
- Who did you ask?
- How informed was the sampled population about this topic?

- What might have happened if you had asked a different group of people?

The Conclusions
- How are your results different from your conclusions?
- What conclusions can't we make?
- How might your choice of a mathematical concept (e.g., ratio, average) influence your audience's thinking?

In the first part of this chapter we examine how the size and experiential background of the sampled population can influence the conclusions one can draw. Later we discuss the importance of distinguishing between results and conclusions. We emphasize how essential it is for children to not only critique their own texts but also the texts of others. Finally we look at how mathematical concepts, such as average and ratio, can be used by authors to frame their argument and position their audiences in particular ways.

The Sample: Who You Ask Can Make a Difference

Remember the 9-year-old described in Chapter 1 who wanted a cell phone for Christmas? She gathered data from family and friends in the hope of convincing her mother to make the purchase. When she began to analyze the data she decided to eliminate the responses of those over 30 years old "because they are really too old to understand what a 9-year-old really needs, and besides, they are messing up my questionnaire!" This young surveyor knew the importance of the sample, and strategically decided to revise her sample to include only those who agreed with her argument.

A similar incident with a sampled population happened to Skip Fennell, past President of the National Council of Teachers of Mathematics. In a NCTM newsletter (Fennell, 2007), he noted that a survey of members showed that the mean age of the membership was 54 years. He had used those data to argue that one of the NCTM's most pressing priorities was to actively recruit younger members to fill the impending vacancies in the ranks of the organization's leadership. However, as he wrote about the importance of interrogating data, he readily admitted that one NCTM staffer did not like his using this piece of data because the average did not reflect the fact that most of the NCTM members did not include their age on the annual survey. Like his 9-year-old counterpart, the President of the NCTM used a narrow sampled population to put forth his particular argument, but doubts were raised about the validity of the conclusions drawn.

Experience, Interests, and Cultural Perspectives of a Sampled Population

The experiences, interests, and cultural perspectives of a sampled population influence the kinds of conclusions that may be drawn as well. In Chapter 4 we described how fifth graders raised questions about a surprising number of negative third-grade responses when asked if they would favor including a daily soup, salad, or sandwich choice on the cafeteria menu. Did the third graders understand the question? Did they have experience with these kinds of menu options? From a critic's perspective, they were asking, "How does the experience (or lack of experience) of the sampled population affect data that are collected?"

At another school, a class of third graders developed similar insights about the sample during a social studies unit on multicultural perspectives (Whitin, 2006). The class composition in this urban school reflected a wide range of ethnicities and nationalities, so the teacher encouraged the children to share their personal cultural knowledge with their peers. Food was a popular topic, and much conversation centered on various ethnic dishes eaten both at home and in the neighborhood's many ethnic restaurants. When their teacher suggested that the children ask other classes about their cultural experiences, it was logical to include the question, "What is your favorite ethnic food?"

After collecting the data, the children categorized the choices by nationality (e.g., spaghetti, lasagna, and pizza as "Italian"). The results included: Italian food, 44; Chinese, 28; Spanish, 10; Mexican, 4; Thai, 2; and Indian, 2. As they discussed their findings, the children realized that they could not draw definitive conclusions about these results. One student wondered if the number of Italian food responses was "because we got a lot of Italian kids at this school." Other children suggested that "a lot of kids have tried Italian food" and "there are a lot of Italian restaurants." These comments seemed to plant some seeds of doubt about the validity of findings. The conversation continued:

- "Not many people picked Indian food or Thai food."
- "But I don't think a lot of people know what Thai food is like."
- "Yeah. We really don't know if people like Thai food if they never tried it!"
- "Some people might vote for one thing because they don't know anything about the other choices."
- "So we don't know if people voted for a food because they really liked it, or because it is from their culture, or they never tried the other foods."

These comments demonstrate several aspects about the nature of a sampled population. What were the experiences of those polled? Were they equally familiar with all of the choices? Was there a relationship between children's cultural identities and their preferences? Raising such issues gave these young children insight into the role that the experiences, identities, and interests of a given sample can play in reported data.

The objections raised by the third graders bear some interesting similarities to those expressed in a letter written to the science editor of the *New York Times* (Friedman, 2009) regarding a reported study about people's buying behaviors

(Tierney, 2009). Conducting their study in an expensive Tel Aviv restaurant, the researchers investigated the effect of providing on a fixed price menu the corresponding à la carte total for each choice. They hypothesized that diners might be influenced by the knowledge of the best value and adjust their choices accordingly. When the results didn't show a high rate for the best value meals, the researchers suggested that the price differences might have been too small to convince the patron. However, in his letter to the editor, Mr. Friedman pointed out that other factors about the sampled population might have contributed to this study's results. At least two of the menu choices were not kosher, and the patrons were likely to have been either ethnic or observant Jews. He continued his argument by emphasizing that food choices of even nonobservant Jews are not easily predicted. Conducting the same study in a different setting with a population that reflected a different set of identities and experiences would likely produce different results. Conclusions cannot be drawn without raising questions about the nature of the sample.

What are the Limits? Distinguishing Between Results and Conclusions

During their study of the school lunch program, the fifth-grade children described in earlier chapters also gained insight into the relationship between the nature of the sample and the conclusions that could be drawn from the results of the data. On this day the children's task was to analyze data from a food preference survey that a representative class from the third, fifth, and eighth grade had completed. They focused on two of the questions that asked respondents to select two out of nine vegetables and two out of nine fruits as favorites. The children worked in pairs to tabulate the results from their assigned grade level. They also noted the sample size for each grade by counting the number of returned surveys. They included this information on bar graphs that represented their results. We then gathered the six children together to consider several ideas before writing about their interpretations and conclusions.

The children were familiar with our customary question, "What does the graph not say?" We decided to use this opportunity to introduce the term "limitations." We asked what associations the children had with the words "limit" and "limitations." They named ideas such as speed limit, time limit, and one child summarized, "It's limited—you can't go over. So, limitations." Building upon her words, David drew a heavy line on the board and said, "So it's like a line that you can't go over. When we look at our graphs, we can't be sure about some things. On one side of the line we're sure about what we can say. On the other side of the line we can't be sure."

Phyllis continued, "What are you limited in saying about your graph? What are your limitations?" Christy pointed out that based on our graph, we couldn't say that the respondents disliked the fruits or vegetables that they didn't circle:

"We're limited by what they didn't choose. It doesn't really mean that they *don't* like the ones they didn't choose." Shaun suggested that perhaps some children hadn't tasted all of the listed fruits and vegetables. Maya agreed: "Maybe they haven't heard of it." As the children conducting the ethnic food survey found, the knowledge and experience of the sampled population influence the conclusions one can draw.

David also reminded the children that when they read the responses from the fifth-grade class (a class with a different teacher), they had disagreed with the choices that the children in the other fifth grades had made. This personal perspective as fellow fifth graders helped them understand the limits of sample size. In this case they could not conclude that the favorites named by *this* third-, fifth-, or eighth-grade class were the favorites of *all* third-, fifth-, and eighth-grade children in the school. David pointed to the line that he had drawn on the board and said, "So for our graph we can say that the information we are presenting is for one third-grade class, but we can't 'go over' [the line or limit] and say that these results reflect the opinions of all third graders. We can't be sure." In this way David built upon the children's language ("go over") and observations about the survey responses to emphasize the difference between results (the number of votes) and the conclusions (implications from these data). Thus, our intentions as teachers were to raise the children's awareness of these distinctions and to provide for them the discourse of critique. Talking together gave the children opportunities to generate and examine ideas.

The children's written reports reflected ideas that we discussed together as well as new observations and analysis. Josiah elaborated on the idea that although the choices indicated favorites, the lack of votes did not necessarily mean dislike: "The interesting thing was that pears, mangoes, and grapefruit were the least favorite. The thing we can't say is that they do not like them because it might not be their favorite fruit. But they still like them." Kevin stated, "The limitation of my graph is that we only asked one class," an idea from the discussion. He then recalled earlier conversations about social expectations to "look healthy," and added, "We're not sure that everyone put their real opinion down. They probably wanted to look healthy." These students' reports showed limitations related to the sampled population's experience, degrees of preference, and awareness of school values and expectations, as well as the sample size.

Christy approached the task from a different perspective. As she prepared to write, Christy imagined what parts of her graph might lead her classmates to draw inaccurate or faulty conclusions. What might they be "not sure about?" Next to the graph she had noted that the sample size was 20, yet the sum of the favorites named was 48 (Figure 5.1). Christy then realized that what was missing was the wording of the question, "Circle one or two choices." She felt that it wasn't fair to withhold this information from her audience.

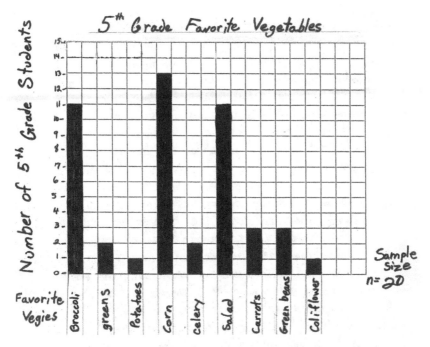

Figure 5.1 Christy's graph of favorite vegetables showing 48 responses from a sample of 20 students.

They would be confused by the discrepancy between the sample size and the total of votes, and they might also conclude that the report was about top favorites only. She therefore wrote in her report, "What didn't show in my graph was that it *didn't* say that some students had two or three choices. Each square does not mean one person. I bet that if people saw the sample size, they would think, 'How [do] all of those squares equal 20 people?' Actually the squares do not represent people. They represent the number of certain vegetables" (Figure 5.2).

These children's experiences have implications for classroom practices that promote a critical orientation toward data. The children were able to develop these insights because the data topic was meaningful, and they were actively involved in tabulating the results, calculating the sample size, constructing the graphs, and discussing their findings. Moreover, they prepared their reports for an authentic social purpose; they knew as they worked that they would be sharing them with their classmates. The responsibility they felt toward their peers underscored the importance of distinguishing between defensible and unfounded conclusions. Christy's experience especially suggested to us that the children were beginning to understand that data reports are not neutral, and that honesty and transparency are important aspects of ethical reporting of data.

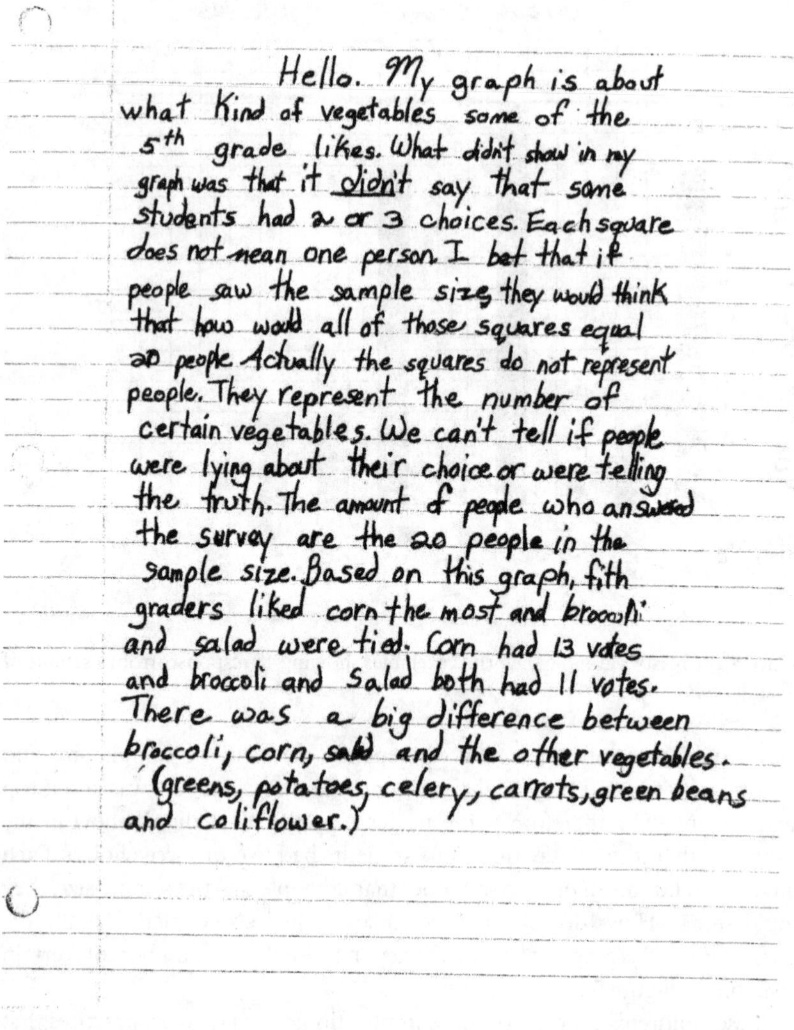

> Hello. My graph is about what kind of vegetables some of the 5th grade likes. What didn't show in my graph was that it _didn't_ say that same students had 2 or 3 choices. Each square does not mean one person. I bet that if people saw the sample size they would think that how would all of those squares equal 20 people. Actually the squares do not represent people. They represent the number of certain vegetables. We can't tell if people were lying about their choice or were telling the truth. The amount of people who answered the survey are the 20 people in the sample size. Based on this graph, fifth graders liked corn the most and broccoli and salad were tied. Corn had 13 votes and broccoli and salad both had 11 votes. There was a big difference between broccoli, corn, salad and the other vegetables. (greens, potatoes, celery, carrots, green beans and coliflower.)

Figure 5.2 Christy's report included a careful explanation about the number of responses and the sample size.

Six-year-olds Grapple with the Issue of Results vs. Conclusions

A class of first graders confronted this same issue of grappling with the distinction between results and conclusions. In an effort to relate a graphing experience to a familiar context, the teacher decided to poll her students about their favorite flavor of milk. She first asked, "What flavors of milk should we use for our graph?" They named chocolate, strawberry, vanilla (plain milk). One child suggested "blueberry." Several children doubted that a blueberry flavor existed, so the class decided instead to add an "other" category. The teacher then distributed a figure of a milk carton to each child, and asked the children to color them with their chosen flavors and glue them on to the class graph.

The task seemed clear enough, but one child raised an issue that was the impetus for the whole class to examine the distinction between results and conclusions. As the children were busy coloring and gluing, Jason quietly approached the teacher and whispered that he had two favorites, chocolate and strawberry, and he didn't know how to show his vote. The teacher asked him how he could solve his problem, and he said, "I know. I'll just color half my milk carton brown and the other half pink." He then placed his tally under "other" since he felt that category was the most appropriate. The final results were: 13 chocolate, 11 strawberry, 0 plain, and 3 other. The teacher then asked, "What do you notice about our graph?" The children observed:

- "I added all of the milks and it was 27."
- "If I put the chocolate with the strawberry it is going to be 24."
- "Chocolate got the most."
- "Strawberry got less and chocolate got more."

Kyle then asked about the milk carton under "other" that had two colors on it. The teacher explained what Jason had done and asked the class if Jason could have placed it somewhere else on the graph instead. Tony remarked, "He can't put it under 'strawberry' because then he's only going to be liking straw-berry," and Anna objected, "And if he puts it under chocolate it will say he only likes chocolate." The children finally decided to place Jason's vote between the strawberry and chocolate columns to show his double preference. The teacher then raised another possibility: "What if we gave Jason two milk cartons to put on the graph?" The children were vehemently opposed to that suggestion: "Then it [the graph] would have a little more chocolate and more strawberry," protested one. "It's not going to be fair because he would have more than us," claimed another. "He should only get one because two would be cheating."

The children were raising the issue of fairness by questioning if one child should be allowed to have two votes. Even Jason was aware that his two votes would have changed the total number of votes cast (thereby creating a mis-match between number of votes and sample size). He wrote in his reflection (Figure 5.3): "If my chocolate and my strawberry, if you put them together it would be 26" (chocolate and strawberry combined was 24). Thus, these first graders raised the issue of power (Jason "would have more than us") as well as the mathematical integrity of the data-collection method. They did not want anyone to be able to conclude from their graph that Jason had more power and privilege than the others.

This whole discussion about Jason's decision to select two flavors, and what to do about it, brought to light the difference between results and conclusions. When the teacher next asked the children, "What does our graph *not* tell us?"

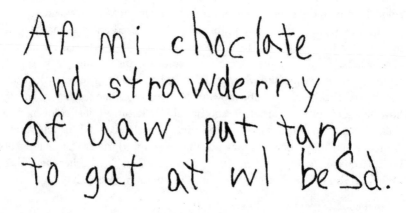

Figure 5.3 Jason attempted to explain how his double vote would change the class data: "If my chocolate and my strawberry, if you put them together it would be 26" (24 + 2 = 26).

she was effectively asking them what conclusions cannot be drawn. The children offered several ideas:

- "It doesn't tell if anyone else likes both chocolate and strawberry the same."
- "It doesn't say if people like two other flavors the same, or maybe three flavors the same."
- "It doesn't say what flavors people don't like."
- "It doesn't tell which one people drink the most" [distinguishing between what is their favorite and what they actually drink most of the time].

Thus, the children's initial observations about the graph focused on the results, but this later discussion about Jason's vote prompted the children to consider some conclusions that they could not make about the data. Even young children can begin to make these distinctions when the data are their own.

Results and Conclusions: Exposing the Partial Story

As children work regularly with data texts they come to understand, as critics, that all such texts are partial. For instance, the first graders realized that they recorded people's first preference for milk but not their second. In the two stories that follow, it is this awareness of what is missing that helps children distinguish between results and conclusions. We also offer an example of a hydrologist who discusses the limitations of longitudinal data reports. As Best (2004) notes, it is an important job of critics to expose the incomplete nature of the reported information: "Something is, in short, always missing.

In evaluating statistics, we should not forget what is lost, if only because this helps us understand what we still have" (p.25).

Andrew was a member of one of the fourth-grade classes that observed birds throughout the year (Whitin, P. & Whitin, D. J., 1997). He learned an important lesson about the incompleteness of data texts when he decided to track the behavior of a bluebird pair that were building a nest outside the classroom window. This example shows how David's questioning helped Andrew confront the many decisions he had to make as a scientist in the field. By responding to David's questions, Andrew made explicit what he was choosing to record and what he was choosing to let go. As he made these moment-to-moment decisions he became aware of the complexity of the data-gathering process. In addition, his reflections about the choices he was making helped him to be a more informed critic later when he made distinctions between his results and conclusions.

Class members had been gathering data about the bluebirds, such as the number of trips the female made to the bird box. Andrew decided that he would track where the female bluebird landed before she flew into the box with nesting material. Before he began he made a four-column data-gathering chart, indicating the four ways that he had previously seen the female enter the box: from the tree; from the top of the school (roof); flying straight in the box; and landing on the box itself before entering (Figure 5.4).

David joined Andrew as he sat by the window and began his observations. Almost immediately unexpected events occurred. David used these opportunities to raise issues Andrew might consider as he recorded his data. For instance, David noted that sometimes the bird landed on one of the four predetermined locations but then was scared away and never went into the box. "Is that something you want to record?" he asked. Andrew decided to note that behavior by placing an "O" by the appropriate landing spot. The next unanticipated problem Andrew faced was that the female sometimes flew to several locations before entering the box. "Are you going to keep track of these different locations or are you going to just record the last stop before entering the box?" David asked. Again Andrew decided to track this behavior as well and marked an "X" for every location that the female used.

The longer Andrew observed, the more he realized that he could not record every behavior he saw. For instance, sometimes the female flew straight into the box by flying close to the ground and at other times she swooped from above. Andrew decided not to record that distinction. He also noted that sometimes the male landed on the box, but he decided to just keep track of the female's behavior. Thus, his visual was the result of a long string of decisions he made along the way.

As indicated on his chart, Andrew's results did show that the most common way for the female to enter the box was to fly straight in; the next most common behavior was to land on top of the box; and the female rarely flew

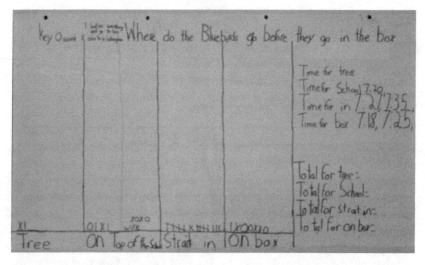

(a)

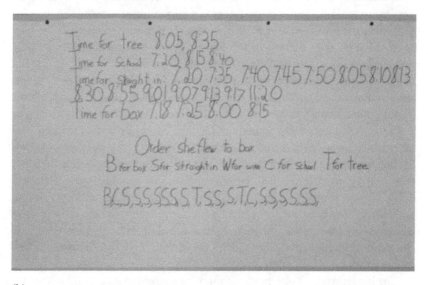

(b)

Figure 5.4a and 5.4b Visual record showing observational data of a female bluebird's visits to the nesting box.

from the tree to the box. Although he could justifiably report these results, Andrew could not draw certain conclusions. For instance, since his recording system did not indicate the sequence of the female's hops from location to location, he could not conclude if a pattern existed whenever the female flew to several locations. In addition, he could not conclude if the male's presence influenced the female's behavior in any way. Thus, Andrew learned that his story, like those of others, was part of a larger story. Like all life scientists Andrew was realizing that the natural world is more complex than he had first imagined, and that data texts are the result of choices that scientists have to make about what to include and what to exclude. These choices impact upon what results can be reported and what conclusions can be drawn.

Learning to Critique the Texts of Others

Andrew's experience illustrates how children's experience as authors gives them an insider's perspective of the limitations of data texts. Conversely, it is important for students to understand that the decisions professionals make as they collect data likewise influence conclusions that can and cannot be drawn. The fourth graders mentioned in Chapter 3 gained this insight as part of their work with Project FeederWatch (Whitin, D. J. & Whitin, P., 1998). The issues that these children raised bear interesting parallels to Andrew's example; both instances entail limitations imposed by the design of the instrument used to gather observational data.

As described earlier, Project FeederWatch involves tracking the flock size of birds visiting feeders over a span of four months. Cornell Lab of Ornithology provides a tally sheet to record data over each two-day observational period. In addition to recording the number of birds, the instrument instructs observers to record the high and low temperatures and the total precipitation over the two-day period. It was the global nature of the data report that later led to the children reaching the kinds of conclusions that could and could not be drawn.

After submitting the final report to Cornell, we suggested to the class that they return to the data sheets and use them to answer other questions of their own about bird behavior. Some children wondered how the range of species that visited the feeders changed from November to April. The data on the tally sheets clearly informed this question. However, other children found that the way the data were recorded prevented them from answering their questions (e.g., Do more or fewer birds come when it rains?) Because they reported data over a two-day span for both precipitation and flock size, they could not draw any conclusions about the relationship between these two variables. They did not know which species and what amount of precipitation occurred on each day. The parameters of Cornell's survey instrument thwarted them in investigating these relationships. As they discussed their frustration, the children acknowledged that the Project FeederWatch data design did fit the Lab's purpose. Nonetheless, the data that were collected reflected only part of a larger story.

Through this experience the children learned that even professional scientists have to make choices about the way data are collected. While Andrew learned to critique his own recording instrument, these students exposed the limitations of a professional survey. To be accomplished critics of numerical information children need opportunities to interrogate texts as both readers and writers.

Children can also benefit from learning about examples in which professional scientists critically evaluate the kinds of conclusions they can draw from data in their fields. We offer an example here that our son Brett, a hydrologist for the National Weather Service, shared with us. Lake Lanier, the primary water source for Atlanta, has had very low water levels in recent years. Brett and a colleague researched the history of water inflow to the lake in order to see if this trend was part of a larger pattern. The lake was formed in 1956 when the Buford Dam was completed. The research team wanted data from a larger span of time, so they used relevant records to estimate how much water would have come into the reservoir (inflow) beginning in 1904 (Whitin & Dobur, 2009).

An examination of this information in graphic form demonstrates how one might draw quite different conclusions depending on the span of time considered. Looking at the portion of the graph from the past 30 years, one sees that there are years of below- and above-average inflow (Figure 5.5). Without the additional 70 years of data, one might underestimate the severity of these droughts. However, when one considers the full 104 years, one realizes that recent low-point years are more often consecutive (two or three in a row), and

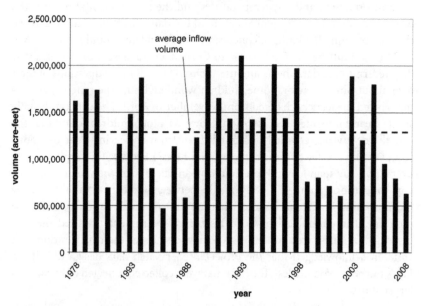

Figure 5.5 Graph of water intake records over 30 years, Lake Lanier, Georgia. Adapted from Whitin, B. & Dobur, J. (2009). An analysis of past significant inflow events into Lake Sidney Lanier. Proceedings of the 2009 Georgia Water Resources Conference, held April 27–29, at the University of Georgia. Public domain.

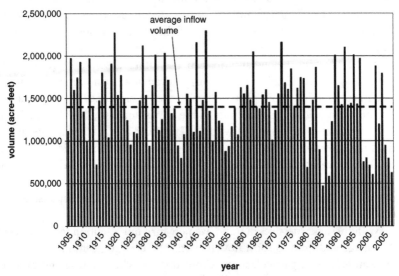

Figure 5.6 Graph of water intake records for 104 years relevant to the area of Lake Lanier, Georgia. Reprinted from Whitin, B. & Dobur, J. (2009). An analysis of past significant inflow events into Lake Sidney Lanier. Proceedings of the 2009 Georgia Water Resources Conference, held April 27–29, at the University of Georgia. Public domain.

the low points are generally much lower (Figure 5.6). Recent droughts are therefore seen to be of unprecedented magnitude. In our conversation with Brett, he further underscored the tentative nature of conclusions drawn from data: "One should wonder how some of these low inflow years in the past couple of decades would stack up against 1,000 years of data. Would droughts look more or less unusual with this additional information?" His example illustrates how professional scientists maintain a vigilant skepticism when drawing conclusions from a given dataset.

This story also shows that when one of the variables in a dataset is time, critics need to ask, "How might the conclusions be different if we used a different time span?" In the following section, we continue this discussion as we examine how the use of other mathematical concepts such as ratio and average impact upon the kinds of conclusions viewers are led to draw.

How the Choice of Mathematical Concepts Frames the Issues

Before we look at the concepts of average and ratio it is important to reiterate how the authoring choices about mathematics, the visual display of data, and language are all intertwined. These three aspects of the data-creation process all impact upon the message because they work together as an orchestrated whole. As authors select, use, and shape one aspect, they inevitably influence the other aspects. For instance, authors can adjust the scale for the visual display of data, as discussed in Chapters 1 and 4. These choices about scale influence the kind of language authors can use to discuss these data. Words like "plummets" and "soars" may be used if the visual is adjusted in particular ways.

As we illustrate below, authors can use either absolute or relative data (which we discuss in this next section) to dramatize or minimize a problem. Their mathematical choice then influences the language they can use to discuss this problem (e.g., "The crime rate in the city is rampant," or "The city is the safest it has been in the past 10 years"). The point is that language about data does not operate in isolation. It is interwoven with mathematical and visual choices. For this reason critics learn to ask, "What mathematical choices did the authors make that allowed them to use this language?" In this way critics can begin to analyze this web of authoring choices and can better understand and evaluate the data for themselves.

With these perspectives in mind, we now turn our attention to the concepts of average and ratio to show how they may be used to position audiences to view an issue in a particular way. Unfortunately, when average and ratio are used in the reporting of a problem or issue, these concepts are often left unexamined; they tend to be interpreted as a given part of the purported problem, rather than as a choice that the author of a text has made. And yet, the concepts that people use to frame a problem are as much a choice as the words in a question or the categories of the data. Such choices involve the art of packaging statistics in a way that best bolsters one's argument (Best, 2008). Let us look at a few examples of how people use these concepts of ratio and average to frame how audiences think about a given problem.

In many instances a number cannot be understood unless it is compared to something else. This comparison is at the heart of a ratio: a comparing of one measure/quantity to another. As such, ratios show relative data as opposed to absolute data. So how can people use these mathematical ideas to their advantage? If one should want to accentuate the seriousness of a flu outbreak, for instance, one can use the absolute data and shout urgently, "5,000 cases of flu-like symptoms have been reported." However, if the number of these cases is compared to an entire city's population, say, 1,000,000 people, then one can minimize the concern by declaring, "The number of reported cases represents only one-half of 1% of the city's population." Each report of the data is correct; but the mathematical expression of those data can either maximize or minimize the significance of that information. In this sense, part of the meaning of what is communicated is embedded in its form of expression. As Elliot Eisner notes, "The form we use to display data shapes its meaning" (Eisner, 2002, p. 12). Thus, it is important for critics to raise questions not only about the message but about the mathematical form (e.g., absolute vs. relative data) which carries that message.

This issue of absolute and relative data came into play when a middle school student, Cara, canvassed her peers about whether they thought it was appropriate for a person to be dating more than one person at the same time. Cara had been perturbed that a former boyfriend of hers had been seeing someone else, and she wondered if more boys than girls thought that this behavior was acceptable. She found that four out of 17 girls and four out of 12 boys thought that such a practice was appropriate. One could argue that the absolute data of four girls and four boys meant that there was no difference in opinion between the two genders. However, Cara argued, "Even though the same number of boys and girls thinks it's okay to date more than one person, I surveyed fewer boys, so that makes a greater percentage than the girls." She calculated that 4/17 girls equaled 24% and 4/12 boys equaled 33%, and therefore a greater percentage of boys approved of this behavior. (Percentages are ratios, as they compare two quantities.) For Cara a ratio, rather than the absolute data, better represented the point she was trying to make.

Informed critics know that data expressed as a ratio was a choice that an author made, and such critics need to ask, "Why did the author choose to represent the problem as a ratio? How would the problem have been perceived differently if it had been expressed in another way?" Another related question that critics need to pose about percentages is "A percentage of what?" Percentages can often hide the actual numbers involved. For instance, what if an ad campaign claimed that 75% of dentists preferred X brand of toothpaste? Such a claim would be an effective form of argument for the X brand. However, what if the ad claimed that three out of a group of four dentists preferred brand X? Now the claim seems less convincing, since the set of dentists interviewed is quite small. Percentages can seem to represent a larger sample than was actually used. Critics recognize this potential problem with percentages and always ask, "percentage of what?"

Critics also know that ratios can provide a context for understanding a problem or issue. Some high school students were complaining about the number of hours they were spending each night doing homework. Some felt "stressed out" and were "exhausted many mornings from staying up so late doing homework." They gathered data on the number of hours some of their peers spent on homework. When they examined the results they believed it was important to express the findings not as absolute data but as a percentage of available hours. If they assumed that there were eight available hours for doing homework (from 3 p.m. to 11 pm), then the amount of hours people were spending on homework (four to six hours) was too much. They calculated that 4/8 up to 6/8 hours per night are spent on homework, or 50% to 75% of students' available time. They felt that 25% (or two hours) was a more reasonable amount of time because it would allow them time to relax, or visit with friends or family.

Since they intended to present these data to their teachers, they felt that the ratio was a better way for them to justify the discrete value of only two hours.

The ratio gave a context and a rationale for understanding why they were proposing this particular amount of time. For these students and others, part of being literate in today's world means choosing and defending which mathematical expressions yield the most convincing arguments. Reflecting on their choices as authors of their own mathematical texts gives children an experiential background for critiquing the choices that other authors have made.

Critiquing the Use of Averages

Just as critics interrogate the use of ratios to persuade and convince, they also need to be vigilant about how people use the concept of average. Critics know that authors of mathematical texts have a choice of three averages: mean, median, and mode. (The mean is obtained by dividing the sum of two or more quantities by the number of those quantities; the mode is the value that occurs most frequently in a dataset; and the median is the middle value in an ordered set of data.) Each type of average can reveal some relationships and conceal others. It is therefore important for critics to ask:

- Why was the mean, median, or mode used to express the data?
- What would the data look like if the average were calculated another way?

One pertinent example centered on President Bush's tax cut proposals (Rosenbaum, 2003). The President claimed that under his plan 92 million Americans would receive an *average* tax reduction of $1,083. However, this average does not tell the whole story. What he failed to mention was that half of those 92 million Americans would have their taxes cut by less than $100, and 78% would get a reduction of less than $1,000. So why was Bush's use of mean as an average so misleading? The large tax reductions to the few rich taxpayers skew the results. For instance, households with incomes of over $200,000 would receive an average tax reduction of $12,496, and for those making over $1 million the reduction would be about $90,222. On the other hand, those with incomes of between $40,000 and $50,000 the tax cut would be $380, and those who made between $50,000 and $75,000 would see a tax cut of $553. The President used an average known as the mean (the total amount of revenue lost divided by the total number of tax returns). The mean (like other statistical measures) can "abstract the particular out of existence" (Eisner, 2002, p. 7).

Critics charged that the President's mean was misleading because the particulars of these tax breaks for most Americans were not made explicit, and were therefore hidden from existence. Calculating the median tax cut would have been a more informative statistic for most people (by rank ordering all the tax cuts and then finding the value in the middle). Of course, even a median cannot express all the particulars for a given population. So critics need to ask, Why is one kind of average being used rather than another? What part of the story is *not* being told? Who benefits from using this particular average?

Opportunities for Children to Interrogate Average

Another of Phyllis's fourth-grade classes learned to interrogate average when they measured seed consumption at their class bird feeder. Over a three-day period they found that 75 cm^3 of seed had been eaten. Wanting to raise the children's awareness of the limitations of expressing the data as a mean, we asked, "If the birds ate the same amount each day [average as mean], how much of that 75 cm^3 would they have eaten per day?" When they answered, "25 cm^3," we continued, "Do we know for sure that it was 25 cm^3 each day?"

One child had reservations about how accurately the mean represented what really occurred. He claimed that birds might be hungrier on certain days, particularly if they were preparing to migrate. As an informed critic he was arguing that this mean did not take into account these kinds of contextual factors. Another child raised doubts about the mean by citing the mathematical improbability of such a number. He argued that the numbers on those three days could have varied widely, such as "10, 65, and 0." He helped his peers to understand that a mean by itself cannot convey the range of numbers that actually occurred in a given total. His observation is similar to the objections raised about President Bush's proposed tax cut benefit. In both cases a wide variability of the data can yield a mean that may be misleading. We as teachers could have capitalized on this child's observation to explore the differences between mean and median. The children might have collected data on seed consumption on a daily basis for three or four weeks. They could then calculate both the mean and the median and compare the results.

Another strategy for engaging children with different types of averages is to give them a set of data and ask them to explain why the mean, median, and mode averages yield such different results. Lappan and her colleagues (1996) suggest one example: Three people are running for mayor in a fictitious town and each has determined the average weekly income for people living in that town. Each candidate is using her data as part of her campaign. Candidate A claims the town is doing very well since the average weekly income is $2,000. Candidate B claims the town is not doing as well as it could because its average weekly income is only $100 per week. Candidate C argues that the town is in miserable shape since the average weekly income is $0! Since none of the candidates is lying and they all used the same set of data, why are their answers so different? A look at some of the town's data reveals an explanation. The town has only 16 residents with the following weekly incomes: $0, $0, $0, $0, $0, $0, $0, $0, $200, $200, $200, $200, $200, $200, $200, $30,600. Children can see that the wide range of incomes can yield vastly different averages: the mean of $2,000, the median of $100, and the mode of $0. Thus, each candidate could portray a different picture of their town based on an average that best supported their argument.

In summary the final section of this chapter highlights how mathematical concepts such as ratio and average are not neutral ideas that are separated from socio-political arguments and debates. Instead, they are in the thick of such discussions because they are tools that authors use to frame a problem and orchestrate an argument. Critics know that authors could have chosen otherwise. They know that there are both advantages and disadvantages to using a particular conceptual frame, and they make explicit what relationships are revealed and concealed. Just as we have argued in previous chapters that the question, categories, definitions, and the visual representation must be questioned, so too does the use of mathematical concepts. And so critics must ask, Why was this scale, average, or ratio used? How would this problem have been viewed differently if another choice had been made? In this way critics come to view mathematical texts as the products of authoring choices and not as unassailable truths.

Next Steps: Strategies for Critiquing the Sample and the Conclusions

This chapter has served to highlight how any set of data is only a partial representation of a problem or issue. The size of the sampled population as well as the knowledge and experience of that population limit what one can say about the data that were collected. Because of the incomplete nature of the categories chosen, the questions posed, and the mathematical tools that were selected, it is important to distinguish between results and conclusions. The examples in this chapter suggest some possible strategies for promoting this critical stance in classrooms.

- *In what ways can children investigate how the size of the sample can influence one's conclusions?*
- *How might children test out questions on different sets of people to see how the knowledge and experience of a sampled population can affect one's results?*
- *In what ways can teachers make children more reflective about the decisions they make about what data to track and what data to ignore? How can teachers use these reflections about the process to help children better critique the data texts found in the media or in textbooks?*
- Some data can be expressed as either absolute or relative (ratio); other data can be expressed as an average: mean, median, or mode. *How might children use this range of choices to frame a given problem, and then discuss or role-play this issue from several different points of view?*
- Children can examine the use of ratio and average in the media and other published sources. *Who benefits from having the data expressed in this way? Who is disadvantaged?*
- There are several ways in which children can begin to understand the distinction between results and conclusions. An analysis of all

aspects of the data-gathering process provides many opportunities to make this distinction. This chapter has highlighted some of these possibilities:

- *Categories*: We knew preferences for milk but not degrees of preference.
- *Questions*: We cannot conclude that one is a favorite if we ask the children to choose two.
- *Sampled population*: Some of the children may not have even tasted Thai food.
- *Visual*: Visuals don't represent everything that happened (e.g., span of time).
- *Social context*: Kids might say one thing but do another.
- *How might teachers capitalize on these various aspects of the data-gathering process to heighten children's awareness of how the choices they make impact upon the kinds of conclusions they can or cannot draw?*

6
Learning to be Critics
A Case Study of Children's Television Advertising

> President Obama says anyone can make a change! So I am trying to do my part. I am asking you to stop advertising unhealthy food on your network.
>
> Derrick, a fifth-grade student

In this final chapter we describe how a critical orientation toward data became an integral part of a long-term inquiry. We collaborated with Kristen and Leslie, the two fifth-grade teachers mentioned throughout the book. We built on our previous year's experiences in which children engaged in an interdisciplinary unit of study of their school lunch program that culminated in an informative presentation for the school board. For this year's project we suggested consumerism as a general topic. Kristen and Leslie agreed that the children would have an interest in and experience with consumerism, and that they might eventually create "smart shoppers" information for their peers. We anticipated that the investigation could incorporate state-mandated curricular content related to mathematics, language arts, economics, and health. We also recognized the topic as one that invites critique. The general framework gave us a place to start, but we all agreed that the children should be involved in shaping the focus of the project. Logistically, we followed our usual format of working with small groups of children each week. The teachers often provided time for these groups to report their findings to their classmates so that all the children were kept informed.

The study ultimately led the children to take social action in the form of writing letters to legislators, manufacturers, and children's television networks, as well as the originally planned presentation for other students. During the project, the children studied marketing strategies, collected data about the content of television advertisements on children's programs, designed a survey to investigate the effects of advertising on the student body, and researched information related to health and nutrition. Throughout the study we strove to empower the children to take on a multimodal, integrated discourse of critique. The children not only learned how marketers use data and language to persuade but they honed their own skills in crafting an argument based on their data-collecting experiences. They critiqued the way sources on the internet reported categories of data, and they exposed the limitations of categories that they themselves devised in analyzing their own data.

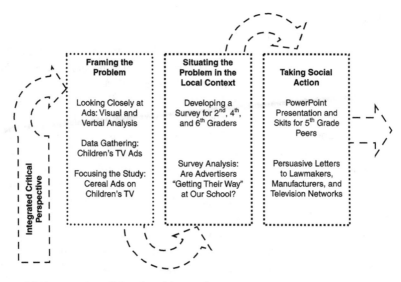

Figure 6.1 An overview of the advertising study.

Figure 6.1 summarizes the evolution of the study. We defined the three phases of the project for the purpose of structuring our discussion rather than to convey a distinct separation of steps; the dotted outlines of the rectangles soften these divisions. The curved arrows represent the integration of principles of critical literacy (Luke & Freebody, 1999) and critical numeracy (Best, 2004; Steen, 2001b, 2007a). The arrows thread through the entire project to symbolize how a critical orientation toward data is an integral part of literacy.

An Initial Interrogation of Marketing Strategies

During the first phase of this investigation we invited the children to look closely at advertising in their daily life. We first asked, "How do advertisers convince people to buy things?" Stephanie noted, "They use a lot of celebrities because people look up to them." Michael observed that advertisers use words like "scariest" to promote movies. Building upon his idea, David drew the children's attention to "-er" words, such as "better than" and "funnier than." Next we asked the children to read selected newspaper ads to see how marketers use these strategies, as well as others, to convince and persuade. After analyzing a few ads together the children worked in pairs, tallying the frequency of words, phrases, and advertising strategies that they saw. The children immediately found examples of comparative language, such as "faster service," "larger pizza," "better tasting," and "easier to read." When we asked, "What do you think of such claims?" they responded that they couldn't tell what these comparisons really meant: "How do you know if it's 'better tasting?' Who is judging it? And how are they judging it?" As critics they were unpacking the ubiquitous advertising strategy known as "the dangling comparative" (Jackson & Jamieson,

2007, p. 31). Such a technique is deceptive because the exact nature of what is being compared is left unclear.

The children also found examples of superlative language, or what has been called "the superlative swindle" (Jackson & Jamieson, 2007, p. 33). Their examples included: "Little Caesars voted best value in America," a mouthwash that was branded as "#1 Dentist Recommended Brand" (an implied "best"), as well as words like "tastiest," "healthiest," "most popular," and "easiest." The children found a claim about a Papa Romano Restaurant that received "Papa Romano's award for three straight years" (again, implying a "best"). We asked the children what questions they would ask the companies about their claims. They replied, "What does 'best' mean? How do they know it's the 'tastiest?' Maybe it's because of all that sugar or salt. Why are dentists recommending this brand of mouthwash? And what do all those awards mean anyway?" Their comments show a critical stance of talking back to the texts. The children were demanding definitions of terms, as well as the criteria for this implied judging and ranking. Figure 6.2 shows additional words and phrases that the children found.

This initial examination of advertisements gave children a heightened sensitivity to how marketers intentionally use language to position people to think and act in particular ways in order to promote their economic agenda (Vasquez, 2004). This insight about language being neither neutral nor impartial is one that the children continued to confront throughout the project.

Investigating Children's Television Advertisements

After this initial examination of newspaper advertisements we asked the children to research TV advertising for homework. We followed Gutstein and Peterson's (2005) suggestions to make a tally sheet for students to record the specific show, channel, kind of product, and brand name (Appendix A). There was also a space for them to make comments. When the children handed in their sheets it was interesting to see that many of the children had noted

Strategy of Advertisers	Examples
Alliteration	Sweet, smart and satisfying; Take-out-taste; Best buy; Heart healthy; Switch on the savings; Pick your pac
Hurry words	All over soon; So little time; Respond asap; Ready tonight; Limited time offer; Now; Expires; Meals in minutes
Repetition	All over the store, all over soon; Good for your body, good for your life; New year, new choices; Real ingredients, real taste; All day, every day
Use of "No"	No trans fat; No high fructose; No artificial flavors; No contract to sign; No limits on minutes; No catches

Figure 6.2 Examples of advertising language in newspapers.

marketing strategies that their peers had found in the newspaper. Already their sensitivity to critique had been raised as they recorded such comments as: "People only get that skin medicine because celebrities use it"; "They use rhyming words to advertise a cooking utensil"; "Tim Horton's used an 'ER' word when it says their coffee tastes 'better' than most coffee."

When we met with four children to analyze the data, we first asked them their thoughts about TV advertising. They noted several important ideas that they pursued later when they focused on cereals. First, they recognized that advertisers know that kids will "pester" their parents to buy their products. Bethany commented: "Kids get grumpy when they can't have things, and companies know that kids will complain to parents." Second, several children noted the connection between advertising and health. Terrel remarked about the ads he had noted on his tally sheet: "The food bothers me. People are getting fat with all the candy, chicken and shrimp. Some people never check on the back to see how much sugar and trans fat there is. And so they'll end up in the hospital dying." Other children expressed similar sentiments, so we decided to graph just the food advertisements. This concern about the marketing of unhealthy foods became a dominant and persistent lens for the entire project.

As the children began to examine the data sheets, they immediately ran into difficulties. The directions had specified children's TV, but several sheets named shows such as *Home Makeover*. Should they count the ads from that show? Christian argued that this show was for families, not just children, and it should not be counted. There was more debate over the show, *Homer 50*. Terrel objected to counting it as a children's show because there was "cussing." Chelsea countered by saying: "The only cuss word that Homer uses is the 'H word.' And if you're going to talk about cussing what about Disney? They have some cussing, like in the 'Ice Princess.' " As critics they were grappling with the definition of what a "kids' show" is. How they defined that word affected which data were counted or omitted. The decision could potentially strengthen or weaken their argument about ads on children's shows. After some discussion they decided to include *Homer* and Disney shows but to exclude other family programs such as *Home Makeover*.

As the children tallied the data, they created categories of advertisements. For food they found 13 cereal ads, 9 restaurants, 3 candy, and 17 grocery items. Within these general categories they identified good and bad foods. For instance, under grocery items the children specified three levels: good foods (yogurt, soup); bad foods (cookies, chips); and partially good (a prepackaged lunch product might have protein but also high fat). They also commented on the high sugar content of many of the advertised cereals.

To build on this interest in refining their categories we found a report on the web that summarized the best and worst cereals as ranked by Consumer Report (Boyles, 2008). This listing, which included 27 of the cereals most heavily marketed toward children, contained categories of "very good," "good," and "fair" (Consumer Report's lowest rating). The criteria for the "very good" category were cited as: no more than 9g of sugar, no more than 210mg of sodium, and at least 2g of fiber. As the children examined the chart we asked them if they agreed with how the cereals were categorized. They were struck by the grouping of Cheerios (1g sugar) and Honey Nut Cheerios (9g sugar) into the same "very good" category. Jacqueline remarked, "There's a big difference between one and nine." They also questioned why Kellogg's Frosted Flakes Reduced Sugar was not in the "very good" category because it had 8g of sugar and 180mg of sodium. We pointed out that the fiber content was less than 1g and reminded them of the "2g" criterion for the "very good" category. (See Appendix B for a chart we developed containing information from this report as well as from other sources.)

Through this discussion, the children began to realize that establishing a ranking system is no simple matter, even for an established agency. Consumer Report made choices in a parallel way to the children's work in categorizing foods for their graphs. Interestingly, the report even acknowledged that there was "room for improvement" in the nutritional content of most cereals. These insights into the decision-making process gave the children confidence to critique aspects of the ranking system of this report, such as the inclusion of cereals with a range of 1–9g sugar as "very good."

As we reflected later about this aspect of the project we realized the important role we played in supporting the children's right to raise questions. There were several factors that worked against the children's adopting a critical stance toward published data-related texts. First, there was the issue of power. What right do children have to question the data from a well-respected agency? Second, there was the issue about the source of the information. Studies have shown that children generally trust information on the internet (Coiro, 2005). So why question "reliable" information? Third, there was the issue of the sanctity of numbers. The data about these cereals were scientifically determined, so how could one disagree? Given these contextual forces we teachers needed to persist in inviting the children to raise questions in order to develop an integrated discourse of critique over time.

Creating Graphs to Summarize the Data

The Consumer Report ratings influenced the way the children decided to make their graphs of the data. Terrel and Christian were appalled that one of the ads featured Apple Jacks, a cereal with 12g of sugar. They decided to add this layer of information about unhealthy foods on their graph by creating a color-coded system. They chose red to symbolize the least healthy foods, orange for the next level, and then yellow. Green represented the healthiest food. They chose these colors because red and orange often represent danger, and they associated green with nature and healthy eating. On their graph they designated the restaurant category as yellow to represent a range of menu choices. Grocery store items were differentiated by various colors depending upon the product. They categorized cereal and candy as either orange or red. The boys then labeled the one "red" cereal "Apple Jacks" so that they could reveal its identity to their peers (Figure 6.3). This graph was thus an integrated, multi-layered representation. Its textual features of numbers, language, and color in a stacked bar graph design worked together multiplicatively to render a stronger argument against unhealthy foods marketed to children (Lemke, 1998).

We then required the children to write an analysis of their findings. In their reports they expressed their increasing concern about marketing directed at children. Terrel concluded his report, "We were surprised that the people who are making these products are worried about selling instead of about the health problems they are causing."

Bethany and Chelsea, who made a pie chart of the data, voiced similar concerns in their reports. Bethany wrote: "It bothers me that the commercials make it [cereals] look so good but they don't say how much sugar or sodium is in it. It hurts me that they know what they are doing, but keep doing it. You are putting your people, friends, and maybe family in danger." It was this

Figure 6.3 Stacked bar graph of TV advertising data showing a range of healthy to unhealthy foods.

intentional deception that bothered the children the most. They realized that they were being positioned by companies, and that such companies did not always have children's best interests in mind.

Further Perspectives on Health Concerns and Marketing Strategies

Since the children showed a strong interest in the information about the nutritional content of cereals, we decided to focus the remainder of the project on cereal advertising. We turned our attention to the health and nutritional concerns of the cereals. We discussed the value of fiber for lowering the risk of heart disease, links between sodium and high blood pressure, and connections between sugar and diabetes. Many children offered their knowledge about these diseases based on their own family members' health issues. For instance, one girl's grandmother often showed her how she read food labels in order to monitor her sodium intake. Another child described how her grandmother checked her blood sugar levels. As the project continued, the children turned to these classmates for their expertise.

One fact from the internet inspired an additional investigation for the children. It was reported that the amount of sugar in Honey Smacks (15g) is 50% of its serving size weight (Boyles, 2008). The children were intrigued by this choice of expressing the sugar content of the cereal as a ratio, which dramatically emphasized the high sugar content. As a result we assisted the children in calculating the percentages of sugar per serving for some other cereals. To show the sugar content in another way the children next used gram weights to measure the specified amount for each of these cereals (absolute data). Figure 6.4 shows a display of the bags for several cereals.

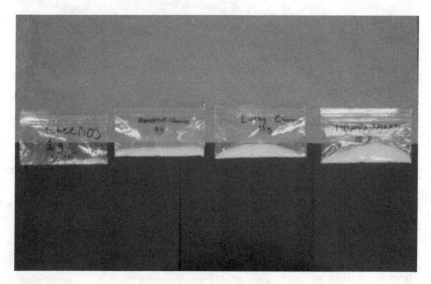

Figure 6.4 Bags of sugar representing sugar content in selected cereals.

The children now had two representations to present to their classmates. One team showed the contrast between two extremes of the "very good" Consumer Report category, Cheerios and Honey Nut Cheerios. They first displayed the bags of sugar that held 1 and 9 grams respectively (absolute data). They then stated that Cheerios had 4% of its serving size weight comprised of sugar, while Honey Nut Cheerios had 33% (relative data). Using these two representations created a convincing argument against the Consumer Report's decision to rank both of these cereals as "very good." The experience with measuring sugar and calculating ratios also helped to underscore that authors of mathematical texts have choices about how data are presented (Best, 2008). It highlighted the critical idea that when concepts such as ratios are used in context, they are strategic tools for building an argument and framing an issue. Thus, they are not value-free mathematical generalizations.

We also discussed marketing strategies related to these health concerns. For example, we shared how companies have changed the names of some cereals over the years (e.g., Corn Pops and Honey Smacks were formerly called Sugar Pops and Sugar Smacks). "Why do you think the companies changed the names?" we asked. The children claimed that "corn" and "honey" gave a healthier impression. Kendell added, "Sugar is not a good thing to have in your title." They realized that although companies changed the names, the cereals continued to have a high sugar content. As critics they were learning how the way one chooses to label a product (or a policy initiative, a war, or an educational program) can influence how others perceive it. Authors use this tactic of persuasion, called "frame it and claim it" (Jackson & Jamieson, 2007, p. 46), to frame an issue or product so that people would view it in a particular way before considering any of the arguments. In response, critics learn to ask, "Okay, that's what they want me to think. Now what's the rest of the story?" (p. 49).

The children further explored this language-related issue when we asked them to compare Frosted Flakes (11g sugar, 140mg sodium, and 1g fiber) with Frosted Flakes Reduced Sugar (8g sugar, 180mg of sodium, and less than 1g fiber). They observed that although the sugar content was reduced, the sodium increased, while the healthy fiber decreased. As critics they were realizing that the label "reduced sugar" was telling consumers only part of the story. Advertisers emphasized specific data for viewers' attention. As Byron remarked later, "The companies are just telling you half the truth." The children were learning that when one hears claims of "reduced," "increased," "lowered," and so on, they have the right to ask, "What else has changed that you are *not* mentioning?"

Although the children criticized the ads for promoting high sugar cereal, many of them admitted that they preferred to eat some of the worst-rated cereals identified by Consumer Report. One student wrinkled her nose as she described the taste of one of the highest rated cereals: "It tastes like grain."

Other children offered explanations for why they preferred some of these lower ranked cereals. In Jade's words, "Kids get used to eating this way." The children realized that they too had been positioned, and that over time advertisers had shaped their own eating habits.

With these reflective conversations in mind, we invited the children to share what they knew about marketing strategies. We borrowed a question that Vivian Vasquez asked her preschoolers when they were interrogating the advertising schemes of McDonald's: "What do companies know about how kids think?" (Vasquez, 2004, p. 125). Derrick described the visual images of children shown in cereal commercials and observed: "Companies make you believe that you can do things, like be good at soccer, or basketball." Dontrell knew that children liked to watch cartoons so that was why cereal companies used cartoon characters like the Trix bunny in their advertisements. Louis and Derrick knew that companies used specific age-related prizes to entice kids, such as toys for younger children, and DVDs and cash cards for older children. Dontrell observed that companies use celebrities to tout their products because children often admire these people. Keandra noted that companies even claim an educational value: "They say on TV that Frosted Mini Wheats make you more focused in school and smarter." Finally, Louis recognized that advertisers know about peer pressure and the bandwagon effect: "Advertisers know that kids talk to kids. They tell their friends. Like if Derrick got a prize in a cereal box and he showed it to us, then we would want one."

The children's observations demonstrated how perceptive they already were in analyzing marketing strategies. We then shared additional information about advertising research (Linn, 2004): Companies employ psychologists to tell them about children's maturational stages of growth and development. They then design advertisements based on this information. For instance, marketers use cartoon characters to talk directly to young children. Developmentally, the youngsters cannot distinguish between fact and fantasy, and are therefore likely to follow the characters' suggestions. Companies also learn about family dynamics from these psychologists and use this information to promote their products. They know that children often determine what gets bought at the grocery store because they will nag a harried parent into buying products advertised on TV. All of this information gave a broader context to what the children had already discussed. It highlighted the intentional and devious manipulation of children for profit.

Researching the Local Context: "Do Advertisers Get Their Way at our School?"

We now felt that the children had developed sufficient foundational knowledge to conduct their own research about the effects of cereal advertising on their fellow students. For this second phase of the project we planned for the children to design a survey for second, fourth, and sixth graders. To create an effective survey, the children needed to pay close attention to both content and design elements, both of which involved a critical perspective.

First, the purpose of the survey guided the content of the questions: To what extent did the marketing strategies for children affect their eating habits? In the words of one child, "Do advertisers get their way at our school?" If so, the long-term health of their classmates might be at risk. Thus, the questions needed to address brands of cereal children eat; who decides what cereals to buy; exposure to cereal ads on TV, and response to marketing incentives such as prizes.

From a design perspective, the children needed to guard against positioning their respondents to answer in a way that favored the fifth graders' agenda. Their role as critics of data-related texts came into play as they considered the survey design and its potential impact on their respondents (e.g., sensitivity to the experience of the sampled population), and the values and expectations implied by the topic, wording, sequence, spatial arrangement, and breadth of choice in answering. An examination of the resulting survey (Figure 6.5) reveals how they had to grapple with these critical decisions.

The direction, "*DO NOT WRITE YOUR NAME ON THIS SURVEY,*" reflects the children's sensitivity to the social context of the event. Two members of the group had responded to the fifth-grade lunch survey from the previous year and recognized the importance of anonymity. Keandra recalled, "Last year we didn't put our name on it." Louis joined in: "If you put your name on it the teacher will know [it's yours]." The children wanted the respondents to feel "comfortable" and not to worry that they might not look like a "healthy kid." We talked about the expectations of parents, teachers, and the school culture itself as factors that could position the respondents. As fifth graders in charge of administering the survey, they too had status and power. So the children agreed that placing the statement in capital letters at the top of the survey would help to ease these social expectations.

The questions about cereal choices and incentives involved decisions about which items to include as well as how to arrange them on the page. For the cereals, the children decided to list only brands that they had seen advertised on TV and that included a range of "very good" to "fair" on the Consumer Report ranking. How to visually present these choices on the actual survey raised some critical issues for the children to consider. Certain spatial arrangements could potentially increase the likelihood of respondents' answering the survey in ways to support the children's desired outcome (e.g., that students at the school are predominately eating high sugar cereals); for instance, listing most of the high-sugar cereals on the top line on the left-hand side, where readers would see them first (Kress, 2000) might influence their peers to select those first. We brought this consideration to the children's attention. Phyllis acted as a recorder on the laptop as the children tried out several alternatives. Together they agreed that

CEREALS THAT YOU EAT   Grade _____

DO NOT WRITE YOUR NAME ON THIS SURVEY

1. Which cereals do you eat most often?   CIRCLE 1 OR 2

Cheerios	Apple Jacks Kix	Froot Loops	Honey Nut Cheerios
Lucky Charms	Reese's Puffs	Fruity Pebbles	Frosted Flakes
Rice Krispies	Trix	Cinnamon Toast Crunch	Other _____

2. Who in your family picks out the cereals?   CIRCLE 1

Me	Adult	Brother/sister	Me and an adult

3. Have you seen TV ads about these cereals?

       Yes   No

What do you notice about the cereal ads you see on TV? _____
_____

4. What makes you most interested to buy a cereal? CIRCLE 1 OR 2

Toy	Game	Taste
Clothes/School supplies	Nutrition	Cash card

Tell more about why you buy these cereals:
_____

5. What do cereal companies know about kids that helps them make their commercials?

Figure 6.5 The Cereal Survey. The questions in bold were included for fourth and sixth grades, but not for second grade.

respondents would be more likely to consider all the choices in a format that interspersed more healthy cereals among the less healthy, the most heavily advertised among the least advertised, and those that the children believed to be the most popular among the least favored cereals. Next they decided to add "other" as a choice; this option was yet another way to gather as accurate data as possible.

The children based the choices for the question about incentives (#4) on their earlier discussion of incentives and games. Drawing on their own experiences with their families, they noted that toys and games appealed to younger children, while older children favored such prizes as cash cards and clothes. Taste and nutrition factored into their decisions at home as well. As Derrick noted, "Me and my mom talk about sweet vs. healthy." The children incorporated these varied reasons on the survey, again arranging the choices to intersperse those that were likely to appeal to younger children among those thought to be attractive to older respondents.

For both questions we asked the children to decide how many options the respondees could select. They thought that the direction "Circle 1 or 2" would give respondents enough freedom to focus on their overall eating habits rather than be confined to a single perceived "favorite." The decisions about space, open-ended response items, and options to choose more than one response all reflected the children's awareness of the power, as well as the potential misuse of power, that rested in their hands as authors.

The children were interested in finding out about the respondents' level of awareness of advertising strategies. We considered three open-ended questions related to this idea:

- What do you notice about the cereal ads you see on TV?
- Tell more about why you buy these cereals.
- What do cereal companies know about children that helps them make their commercials?

The children commented that this last question was appropriate for older children, but not for second graders. With this thought in mind, they decided to differentiate this part of the survey according to age (see Figure 6.5). The second-grade survey included only directions for circled responses. This aspect of the survey design demonstrated the children's sensitivity to the different levels of expertise of the sampled populations.

Designing the survey was a complex task. As critics the children had to consider many aspects of the question: the wording, sequence, open vs. closed format, spatial arrangement, and the limits of a survey given in paper form. They needed to analyze their influence as authors, their status as survey administrators, and the implicit expectations and values of the school context. They accounted for the differing levels of knowledge and experience of the proposed sampled populations. The analysis of the completed surveys would raise new issues to consider as well.

Analyzing the Surveys

Throughout the project we talked with the children about the opportunity to take social action about the problems that they were investigating. We now told them that, together with their teachers, we had made plans for two ways to reach out to others: an informative PowerPoint and skit for the other fifth-grade classes, and persuasive letters to agencies related to the marketing industry. Knowing that the results would be reported to these different audiences enhanced the children's sense of purpose as they set to work. They were not only eager to find the results; they were also committed to tabulate and present their findings as accurately as possible.

Four pairs of children each analyzed data from one of the survey questions, displayed their results in graphical form, and wrote a narrative commentary. Overall, the results confirmed the children's hypotheses:

- The top three cereals named as "most often eaten" had 12g, 9g, and 10g of sugar.
- Most children help to choose the cereals they eat.
- Over 80% of the respondents said that they saw TV advertisements for the cereals named on the survey.
- Taste was cited most often as a reason to buy cereal. Taken together, toys and games carried about as much influence as nutrition. Second and fourth graders chose toys, but sixth graders did not. Children of all ages picked cash cards.

Although the children found these results to be strong evidence, they also realized that there were gaps and ambiguities in the data that left a margin of error. Throughout the tabulation process the children found that their decisions ultimately placed limitations on their conclusions. For example, Jelan and Deon found that a sixth grader wrote "Hannah Montana" cereal in the "other" blank, and they wondered if that cereal would have been chosen by other, older children if it had been specifically listed. Did the choices that were listed restrict or help the respondents? Were differences among age groups lost by these choices? Dilemmas like this one underscored for the children that their data, like those of others, only told a partial story.

The topic of aggregated and disaggregated data arose when the children prepared graphs and wrote their reports. Leilah and Jade, who compiled the data about children's role in choosing cereals, wanted to make a pie chart to display their information. David guided them in converting the raw data to percentages, and the girls included both forms of information on their chart. Almost 50% of the responses were "me and an adult," while "me" had 25%, "brother or sister" had 14%, and "adult" had 13% (Figure 6.6). As they reviewed their work, David asked, "How many responses included kids in some way?" Together the girls noted that three of the categories included children; only the category "adult" excluded them. Thus, the data could be aggregated into two categories: decisions involving adults only and decisions involving children.

Jade included this strategy of aggregating the child-related categories when she wrote her report: "In our graph 87% of the children had a say-so on which cereal they eat. That's why advertisers bring out a lot of bribes knowing children has [sic] a big say-so so they would buy their cereal. The ads would change if [the companies] knew adults had more say-so." Although she kept the finer categories in the pie chart, collapsing the data into two categories in her written report allowed Jade to make a more convincing argument about children's decision-making role. We later wondered if the attention that David brought to the aggregated data also encouraged Jade to think further about how marketers

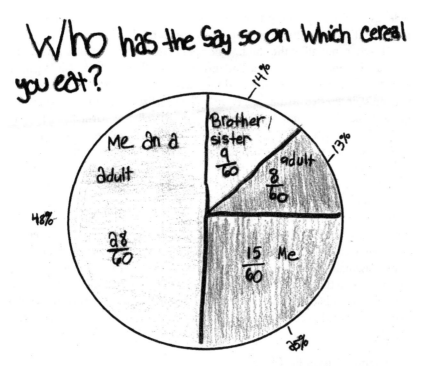

Who has the Say so on Which cereal you eat?

Me an a adult 28/60 48%

Brother / sister 9/60 14%

adult 8/60 13%

15 Me 60 25%

Figure 6.6 Pie chart showing data from the survey question, "Who in your family picks out the cereals?"

might shape their advertisements if they knew adults were the ones who had the most control over cereal purchases.

As Jade's example shows, working with the surveys also gave the children additional opportunities to critique the texts produced by the marketing industry. Their comments indicated to us that they were becoming confident critics. For example, while talking about prizes, games, and other child-targeted incentives, the children mentioned that they were often directed to go online to "see if you win." Thoughtfully, Jelan commented, "And sometimes when you go online a survey pops up." Her insightful observation suggested to us all that here was another strategy marketers used to gather information about children's interests to include in their ads.

Reading the open-ended comments on the surveys prompted Jade to make a connection to an incentive that was not mentioned by any respondent, "Box Top for Schools." Under this program children bring cereal box tops which the school can then redeem to purchase materials and supplies. Jade suddenly realized that this program, too, was a marketing strategy. She analyzed how the social context of the school legitimizes this company program for children because "you would have a good feeling helping out your school." In this way

Jade cast a critical eye beyond toys, games, and other prizes advertised on TV to the institutional incentive program at her own school.

Of course, not all of the children noticed these subtler forms of persuasion such as the box top program. For instance, Jonathan and Mariah began to talk about "games" as they analyzed the results for the question, "What makes you most interested to buy a cereal?" They realized that this category was quite broad; it was impossible to know about all the particular kinds of games that attracted various children. Mariah then remarked that some were "brain games," and suggested that these games have more value than some of the others. Unlike Jade, Mariah did not recognize that the use of terms such as "educational" or "brain-based" were also words chosen intentionally to persuade.

In any case, all of the children were excited about helping their peers be "smart consumers" and encouraging them to express their views to agencies and lawmakers. Michael even incorporated a call for action into his data report to his classmates. He wrote, "We have an assignment for you. Write a letter to companies [so that you can] help children." We agreed that the children knew the issues. They had the data. However, before they started this next step we felt that they needed specific information on ways in which citizens can effect change.

Developing a Vision for Change

In order to give children a vision of what that social action could accomplish, we shared some information which gave them a greater context for viewing their own data. We discussed how some countries, such as Sweden, Norway, and the province of Quebec in Canada, have passed laws that ban all advertising during children's television shows. We added that the United States once had laws that restricted advertising toward children, but in 1984 those laws were changed to allow companies more freedom. David shared that companies want to advertise to children to establish "product loyalty" and create a "cradle-to-grave" consumer (Linn, 2004).

Chelsea suddenly exclaimed, "Can't Barack Obama do something about the ads?" Nodding, Jade added, "President Obama might sign a law because he has daughters, and he doesn't want his daughters to be hooked on this 'cradle-to-grave' stuff. He wants his daughters to be healthy." We agreed, and connected this comment to the vegetable garden Michelle Obama had recently created with the help of fifth graders. Jade continued her argument: "If the President just signed a law then everyone would be helped. Then we could scratch our name off for being one of the most obese countries."

We explained that President Obama could not pass a law by himself. We discussed how laws are proposed and passed, and noted that the legislative branch was designed to represent the interests of the citizens in their districts. We explained that laws can change, and cited the ban on advertising cigarettes on television as another example. Adrian felt especially hopeful about initiating this change in advertising when he wrote in his reflection later: "It's possible for kids to change laws by getting through to the President. Obama doesn't just believe in helping the rich, but everyone." With this vision in mind, the children turned to the tasks of advocating for change through an informative PowerPoint and a letter-writing campaign.

Taking Action: Information for Peers

Eight children worked over two days to design the PowerPoint slideshow. The question, "What is important to tell other fifth graders about TV ads for cereal?" guided the development of the content and sequence of the piece. Their peers' health was foremost in the children's minds. In Adrian's words, "I want to say to children that if we don't stop piling on the sugar then we will get sugar diabetes." The children agreed that if their peers had access to information about marketing and nutrition, and if they understood the impact of advertising on the children in their own school, they could be persuaded to join them in their letter-writing campaign. The resulting outline included:

- Data from the TV viewing project: one-third of ads viewed featured cereal (mostly high in sugar).
- Marketing strategies.
- Nutrition information: sugar, sodium and fiber
- The Cereal Survey: advertisers are "getting their way at our school."
- Laws can change: Take action!

Logistical matters also contributed to the project design. Although we only had one laptop, we wanted to give the children exposure to digital composing. The children had limited experience with technology; none had worked with PowerPoint software. Making an effective PowerPoint would give them experience in building an argument through multiple modalities (e.g., language, images, and animation). This insider's view of multimodal persuasion might also deepen their ability to critique marketing texts.

We asked the children to work individually or in pairs on specific topics from the outline. We based these assignments on the areas of interest that they showed during the project. For example, Amber was knowledgeable about high sodium foods, such as soup, since she often talked with her grandmother, who had high blood pressure. Amber eagerly assumed the responsibility to compose an informative slide about this health-related topic. Adrian, who was concerned with "piling on the sugar," wanted to work on a slide about high and low sugar cereals. Jade had tabulated the survey results about children's purchasing power, so she and a partner composed a slide about these findings. Thus, children brought specialized knowledge to the task.

Before the children set to work, Phyllis showed them a partially completed demonstration slide about marketing incentives. The children discussed compositional choices (e.g., title, use of space, short text, and the animation scheme). Amber suggested adding another image, and together the children chose an appropriate entrance effect. When Jade commented that the show "is designed by kids for kids" her words became part of the title slide. Next the children drafted their own slides on paper, noting the entrance sequence of text and images. For most of the slides Phyllis translated their drafts into digital form, and the authors worked with her on revisions and refinements. When time allowed, the children played a larger role in this step.

Examples of their work demonstrated ways in which the children made their points through words, numerical information, size, color, space, and animation. Adrian contrasted the sugar content of Honey Smacks and Cheerios. He titled his slide "Cereal Science," a choice with an authoritative tone. He added images of a skull and crossbones and a muscular man to emphasize his point, and noted the entrance sequence. Figures 6.7 and 6.8 show his draft and final slide. For their slide, Jade and Jelan decided to feature the aggregated data about children's influence on cereal purchase. A large "87%" occupied the top center portion of the slide to capture the viewer's attention, with "Kids have the say-so on which cereal to eat" written beneath. They gave the disaggregated data in the four corners of the slide, a decision which showed their commitment to their audience not to withhold information. In other slides, the children used red to convey danger or warning. Appendix C shows the completed PowerPoint.

Teachers of writing have asserted for decades that writing informs reading, and reading informs writing (National Council of Teachers of English, 2004; Portalupi & Fletcher, 2001). Similarly we suspected that this authoring of multimodal texts worked to sharpen the children's critique of TV advertising. During the composing process, several children offered new insights about advertisers' design choices. We suspected that the children's active involvement in the creation of their own images heightened their awareness of the power that these images carry, prompting them to reflect on the images they had seen on television. For instance, Jade remarked on a subtle difference between advertisements for regular Cheerios and Honey Nut Cheerios that exposed marketers' intentional choices to target the latter for children. The ad for the sweeter cereal featured an animated bee that would pique children's interest, but the plain Cheerios had no cartoon character. Jelan also noted, "On TV everybody eating [cereal] is skinny," thus recognizing that powerful visual messages such as these positioned viewers not to think about health risks associated with obesity. The children were recognizing the misleading nature of these visual images and were learning: "A picture can indeed be worth a thousand words—but those words aren't necessarily true" (Jackson & Jamieson, 2007, p. 55). These examples show the importance of examining all representational modes with a critical eye (Janks, 2010).

Figure 6.7 Draft of PowerPoint slide contrasting cereals with high and low sugar content.

Back in the classroom, Leslie and Kristen invited interested children to create skits that incorporated mock advertisements as well as information about nutrition and marketing by following the guidelines below:

- Include at least one attention-getting strategy.
- Include one reference to health and nutrition.

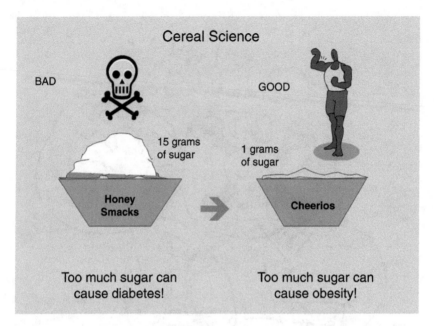

Figure 6.8 Finished PowerPoint slide, entitled "Cereal Science".

- Use language that is engaging and which sounds like an ad.
- Show a "behind the scenes" look that gives the other side of the ad. This analysis can be a part of the ad or follow it.

The children composed, rehearsed, and auditioned. The teachers selected groups to perform their skits as interest-getting introductions to the PowerPoint presentation.

Taking Action by Writing Letters

The children's work on the PowerPoint presentation and their skits gave them an opportunity to summarize the main points of their investigation and to rehearse their argument for change. We assembled and gave a list of those key points to the teachers, Kristen and Leslie. After talking with the children about possible audiences for their letters, such as their congressional representatives, cereal companies, and television programs, we researched addresses for the children to use. With this information to hand the teachers then involved the children in this letter-writing campaign. Chelsea's letter to the Kellogg's Company reflects many of the issues that were most troublesome to her: high sugar contributing to serious diseases; companies using bribes to persuade, and manipulating sugar/sodium content to "maintain taste." As a critic she described the problem, exposed the tactics that the company uses to position consumers, and then argued that the situation could be otherwise if companies chose to think seriously about health implications. She wrote:

I am writing this letter to inform you that your cereal is too high in sugar or sodium. Cereals advertised on children's television shows lead to heart problems, diabetes and obesity. Likewise most companies use bribes to persuade children to buy their products. Some of these bribes include toys, cash cards, and clothes by mail.

Do you know there are some countries that don't allow advertising to children? Some examples are Sweden and Quebec. Also, these countries don't allow advertisements because your body don't [*sic*] require added sugar. You have enough from fruit. In these countries people are not as obese as people in the U.S.A. because they are not advertised bad foods.

I've learned that many cereal companies will lower sugar and add more salt or vice versa to try and maintain taste. However, I suggest lowering both sugar and salt. This would make these cereals healthier. In closing, thank you for taking the time to read this letter. I believe more people would buy your product if you lower the sugar and salt. That would save the country from being the most obese country. Also it would save people from having the problems they have now.

Apryl wrote to her Congressperson to argue for change. In her letter she informed him of the problem, and discussed some of the positioning techniques that advertisers use. She concluded, "Did you know that companies advertising these unhealthy cereals bribe children to buy their product by using famous people or children's favorite cartoon characters? In closing I believe that cereal companies should not be allowed to advertise unhealthy cereals on children's television." Terrel also wrote this same representative and cited the rise in obesity levels to support his argument: "Over the years the obesity level has doubled since 1970. This rise is due to unhealthy eating habits. I believe laws should be passed to stop unhealthy cereal advertisements on children's television."

Jelan wrote Viacom, the company that produces the show *Nickelodeon*. She urged the company to "stop advertising unhealthy cereals to children" because "some kids don't know that [what] you advertise on your network has a lot of sugar. Many think that cereal is good for you but these [sugar] cereals can cause people to have diabetes." As a critic she wanted to expose how companies prey upon the vulnerability of children. Her comment that people "think that cereal is good" shows how companies use the halo effect (Linn, 2004), a strategy we had discussed with the children. Since breakfast is a healthy morning routine, companies use that halo of good health to position consumers to buy their products. Finally, Derrick connected his efforts to halt this advertisement of sugar cereals to President Obama's call for everyone to become agents of change. Part of his letter to Viacom stated: "President Obama says anyone can make a change! So I am trying to do my part. I am asking you to stop advertising unhealthy food on your network."

About six months later General Foods announced that it was planning to reduce the amount of sugar in cereals that it markets to children (Associated Press, 2009, p. B1). The announcement came amid "growing scrutiny from consumers, regulators and health groups over the nutritional value" of many foods (p. B1). Although we were no longer meeting with the children, we sent the newspaper article to Leslie and Kristen so that the former fifth graders could see that their voices were among those that had protested against these unhealthy products and made a difference by doing so.

However, given the research that they had done on sugar content, the children would most likely reserve judgment about General Foods' decision until the final product was available for inspection. Although the company intended to decrease the sugar levels to single digits in 10 of its cereals, we are quite certain that these children would ask, "What are you going to do with the levels for sodium and fiber?" The children's research had revealed that companies manipulate all three of these variables, often increasing sodium and decreasing fiber, to maintain taste. As text critics they knew to dig beneath the surface of showy headlines and official proclamations to examine what is said and not said, and to raise additional questions for consideration.

Looking Back on the Investigation

The stories in this chapter demonstrate the integration of critical literacy and critical numeracy in a long-term inquiry. There were numerous aspects of this integration. First, the children's work showed the natural integration of language, mathematics, social studies, art, ethics, and psychology. It highlighted how mathematics cuts across all of these fields, emphasizing that every teacher needs to be a teacher of mathematics (Steen, 2007a). The consumerism project also showed the integration of skills and concepts but always with a critical perspective. The children analyzed the potential of and drawbacks to expressing their argument by means of absolute or relative data, or a pie chart versus a bar graph, or aggregated or disaggregated data. They examined how marketers use comparative and superlative language to persuade. As the children composed their survey and PowerPoint presentations, their work highlighted another instance of integration (e.g., how the form of their communication was also a part of their overall message) (Eisner, 1994; Kress, 2000, 2003). They analyzed their symbolic use of color, the organization of spatial elements, and the utilization of animation, and viewed these decisions as essential features for effectively conveying their argument.

The children's work also showed the integration of critical attitudes and dispositions across the curriculum. These fifth graders were willing to postpone judgment, feel comfortable with uncertainty, and be confident in questioning an established authority. Finally, this project exemplified the integration of research and action. Once the children had done their research they used their findings to inform their peers, and to urge governmental and corporate agencies to change their policies.

This consumer project underscored the central role that teachers play in promoting a discourse of critique. By raising the kinds of questions outlined in our heuristic (Figure 1.1) we heightened children's awareness about the ways that marketers position them to think and act. Questions became the catalyst for interrogating language, questioning ranking systems, and exposing corporate motives. The multimodal nature of texts of the twenty-first century demands a critical stance not just toward language, but toward mathematics and the visual elements of design. It is a stance that can empower our students to analyze and address the issues of our increasingly complex world.

Appendix A
Investigating Commercials on Children's Television Shows

Directions: Watch one or more shows on a popular children's television channel. Fill in the information about your observation times. During the shows, every time there is a commercial, watch it carefully and record information about it on the chart. Use extra paper if you need it.

Day and Time of Observation	
Total number of shows watched	
Total amount of time spent watching the shows	

Show and Channel		Time (For example, 9–9:30 Sat. AM)
Kind of Product (food, game, etc.)	Brand Name	Any comments you want to add

Based on Gutstein, E. & Peterson, B. (Eds.). (2005). *Rethinking mathematics: Teaching social justice by the numbers.* Milwaukee, WI: Rethinking Schools.

Name of Cereal	Sugar	Sodium	Fiber	Serving Size
Rated "Very Good"				
Cheerios	1 gram	210mg	2 grams	28 grams
Kix	3 grams	210mg	3 grams	
Life (Quaker Oats)	6 grams	160mg	2 grams	
Honey Nut Cheerios	9 grams	190mg	2 grams	28 grams
Rated "Good"				
Kellogg's Frosted Mini-Wheats	12 g.	5mg	6 grams	59 grams
Kellogg's Frosted Flakes Reduced Sugar	8 grams	180mg	<1	31 grams
General Mills Cookie Crisp	11 grams	150mg	1 gram	
Golden Grams Honey Grahams	11 grams	270mg	1 gram	
Lucky Charms	11 grams	190mg	1 gram	
Cocoa Puffs	12 grams	150mg	1 gram	
Cinnamon Toast Crunch	10 grams	220mg	1 gram	30 grams
Trix	12 grams	190mg	1 gram	32 grams
Reese's Puffs	12 grams	180mg	1 gram	29 grams
Kellogg: Frosted Flakes Gold	10 grams	190mg	3 grams	
Frosted Flakes	11 grams	140mg	1 gram	30 grams
Cocoa Krispies	12 grams	160mg	1 gram	
Post: Fruity Pebbles	11 grams	180mg	3 grams	
Honey-Comb	11 grams	220mg	2 grams	29 grams
Cocoa Pebbles	11 grams	180mg	3 grams	
Lowest Rating (Fair)				
Kellogg's Honey Smacks	15 grams	50mg	1 gram	27 grams
Post's Golden Crisps	14 grams	25mg	1 gram	
Cap'n Crunch's Peanut Butter Crunch	9 grams	200mg	1 gram	
Cap'n Crunch (Quaker Oats)	12 grams	200mg	1 gram	
Kellogg: Apple Jacks	12 gram	135mg	<1 gram	28 grams
Froot Loops	12 grams	135mg	<1 gram	29 grams
Corn Pops	12 grams	110mg	0	29 grams
Rice Krispies	4 grams	220mg	0	

Notes

Cereals with missing serving sizes were listed by cup measure rather than weight in grams.

The recommended maximum daily sodium intake is 2300 mg, or about the amount in a teaspoon of salt.

The cereals with less than a gram of fiber (<1 gram) are rated as 0% RDA (Recommended Daily Allowance).

Sources

Boyles, S. (2008, October 1). Kids' cereals: Some are 50% sugar. Retrieved from http://www.webmd.com
www.dietfacts.com

What You Should Know about Cereal Ads on TV

Designed *by* kids *for* kids

We researched commercials on kids' TV.

1/3 of the ads were for cereal . . .

and most of the cereals have a lot of sugar!

Cereal Companies Use Special Tricks to Impress Kids

 TOYS

 Cash Cards

 Games

Cartoon Characters

Advertisers know that kids have a lot of say-so about which cereal they eat.

But most of the cereals rated "very good" aren't advertised on kids' TV.

Here's what we learned that ads DON'T tell you.

Cereal Science

BAD

15 grams of sugar

Honey Smacks

→

GOOD

1 gram of sugar

Cheerios

Too much sugar can cause diabetes!

Too much sugar can cause obesity!

Other Foods Have the Sugar You Need

Don't eat too much sugar!

 Apple Jacks

What happens when too much sodium enters your body?

Many cereals have a lot of sodium.

High sodium can cause high blood pressure.

Your heart will have to work extra hard.

Read the labels on your cereal boxes!

You only need about 1 teaspoon of salt a day!

Did you know....

... that "reduced sugar" cereal isn't always better for you?

Regular Frosted Flakes — 11 grams of sugar

Frosted Flakes Reduced Sugar — 8 grams of sugar

But when the sugar is decreased...

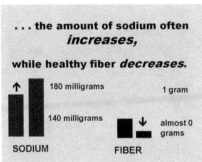

... the amount of sodium often *increases,*

while healthy fiber *decreases.*

180 milligrams   1 gram

140 milligrams   almost 0 grams

SODIUM   FIBER

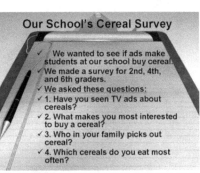

Our School's Cereal Survey

✓ We wanted to see if ads make students at our school buy cereal.
✓ We made a survey for 2nd, 4th, and 6th graders.
✓ We asked these questions:
✓ 1. Have you seen TV ads about cereals?
✓ 2. What makes you most interested to buy a cereal?
✓ 3. Who in your family picks out cereal?
✓ 4. Which cereals do you eat most often?

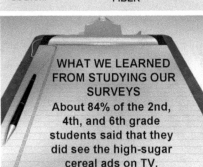

WHAT WE LEARNED FROM STUDYING OUR SURVEYS
About 84% of the 2nd, 4th, and 6th grade students said that they did see the high-sugar cereal ads on TV.

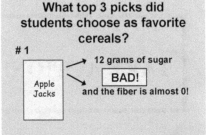

What top 3 picks did students choose as favorite cereals?

1

Apple Jacks

→ 12 grams of sugar

→ BAD! and the fiber is almost 0!

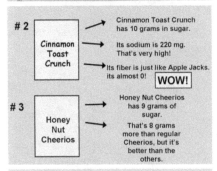

2

Cinnamon Toast Crunch

→ Cinnamon Toast Crunch has 10 grams in sugar.
→ Its sodium is 220 mg. That's very high!
→ Its fiber is just like Apple Jacks. its almost 0! WOW!

3

Honey Nut Cheerios

→ Honey Nut Cheerios has 9 grams of sugar.
→ That's 8 grams more than regular Cheerios, but it's better than the others.

87% of kids have a say-so on what cereal their family buys.

25% "me"

48% "me and an adult"

13% of parents have all the say-so

14% "brother or sister"

13% "an adult"

Apple Jacks

This is why advertisers are advertising on kids' TV shows.

WARNING !!!

ADVERTISERS ARE GETTING THEIR WAY AT OUR SCHOOL!

It doesn't have to be this way.

Laws can change.

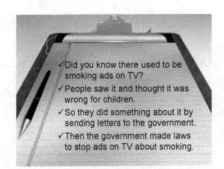

References

Alsup, J., Emig, J., Pradl, G., and Tremmel, R. (2006). The state of English education and a vision for its future: a call to arms. *English Education*, 38(4), 278–295.

Apple, M. (1992). Do the standards go far enough? Power, policy, and practice in mathematics education. *Journal for Research in Mathematics Education*, 23(5), 412–431.

Associated Press. (2009, December 9). General Mills reducing sugar in kids' cereal. *New York Times*. Retrieved from http://www.nytimes.com

Best, J. (2001). *Damned lies and statistics*. Berkeley, CA: University of California Press.

Best, J. (2004). *More damned lies and statistics*. Berkeley, CA: University of California Press.

Best, J. (2008). *Stat-spotting: A field guide to indentifying dubious data*. Berkeley, CA: University of California Press.

Bishop, A. (1991). *Mathematical enculturation*. Boston, MA: Kluwer.

Boaler, J. (2008). *What's math got to do with it? Helping children to learn to love their least favorite subject–and why it's important for America*. New York: Viking.

Borasi, R. (1989). Olympic medal counts: A glimpse into the humanistic aspects of mathematics. *Arithmetic Teacher*, pp. 47–52.

Borasi, R. (1992). *Learning mathematics through inquiry*. Portsmouth, NH: Heinemann.

Borasi, R., & Siegel, M. (2001). *Reading counts: Expanding the role of reading in mathematics classrooms*. New York: Teachers College Press.

Boyles, S. (2008, October 1). Kids' cereals: some are 50% sugar. Retrieved from http://www.webmd.com

Burros, M. (2007, January 9). Bias is found in food studies with financing from industry. *New York Times*, p. A15.

Carey, B. (2009, May 4). Stumbling blocks on the path of righteousness. *New York Times*. Retrieved from http://www.nytimes.com

Cohen, P. (2009, July 8). Mapping a bird's-eye view of foreclosure misery. *New York Times*, pp. C1, C7.

Coiro, J. (2005). Making sense of online texts. *Educational Leadership*, 6(2), 30–35.

Cope, B., & Kalantzis, M. (eds) (2000). *Multiliteracies: Literacy learning and the design of social futures*. London: Routledge.

Curcio, F. (2001). *Developing data-graph comprehension in grades k-8*. Reston, VA: National Council of Teachers of Mathematics.

Derbyshire, D. (2007, January19). Colgate gets the brush off for "misleading" ads. Retrieved from http://www.tetegraph.co.uk/news/main.jhtml?xml=/news/2007/01/17/ncolgate117.xml

Eisner, E. (1994). *Cognition and curriculum reconsidered* (2nd edn). New York: Teachers College Press.

Eisner, E. (2002). What can education learn from the arts about the practice of education? *Journal of Curriculum and Supervision*, 18(1), 4–16.

Ernest, P. (1989). *Mathematics teaching: The state of the art*. New York: Falmer.

Fairclough, N. (2000). Multiliteracies and language: orders of discourse and intertextuality. In B. Cope & M. Kalantzis (eds) *Multiliteracies: Literacy learning and the design of social futures* (pp. 162–181). London: Routledge.

Fennell, S. (2007, September). Take a look at the data. *NCTM News Bulletin*, 44(2), 3.

Freppon, P. (2001). *What it takes to be a teacher*. Portsmouth, NH: Heinemann.

Friedman, R. (2009, July 7). The lure of a bargain. [Letter to the Editor] *New York Times*, p.D.4.

Gee. J. (1992). *The social mind: Language, ideology, and social practice*. New York: Bergin & Garvey.

Gee, J. (1996). *Social linguistics and literacies: Ideology in discourses* (2nd edn). London: Taylor & Francis.

Gee, J. (1999). *Introduction to discourse analysis*. New York: Routledge.

Gutstein, E., & Peterson, B. (eds) (2005). *Rethinking mathematics: Teaching social justice by the numbers*. Milwaukee, WI: Rethinking Schools.

129

Huff, D. (1954). *How to lie with statistics.* New York: W.W. Norton.

Jackson, B., & Jamieson, K. (2007). *Unspun: Finding facts in a world of disinformation.* New York: Random House.

Janks, H. (2010). *Literacy and power.* New York: Routledge.

Jewitt, C., & Kress, G. (2003). *Multimodal literacy.* New York: Peter Lang.

Kagay, M., & Elder, J. (1992, August 9). Numbers are no problem for pollsters, words are. *New York Times.* Retrieved from http://www.nytimes.com

Kress, G. (2000). Multimodality. In B. Cope & M. Kalantzis (eds) *Multiliteracies: Literacy learning and the design of social futures* (pp. 182–202). London: Routledge.

Kress, G. (2003). Genres and the multimodal production of "scientificness." In C. Jewitt & G. Kress (eds) *Multimodal literacy* (pp. 173–186). New York: Peter Lang.

Lappan, G., Fey, J., Fitzgerald, W., Friel, S.,& Phillips, E. (1996). *Data about us.* Connected Mathematics Project. Palo Alto, CA: Dale Seymour.

Lemke, J. (1998). Multiplying meaning: Visual and verbal semiotics in scientific text. In J. Martin & R. Veel (eds) *Reading science* (pp. 87–113). London: Routledge.

Leonhardt, D. (2008, March 5). Unemployed, and skewing the picture. *New York Times,* p. C1.

Leu, D.J. Jr., Kinzer, C.K., Coiro, J.L., & Cammack, D.W. (2004). Toward a theory of new literacies emerging from the internet and other information and communication technologies. In R.B. Ruddell & N.J. Unrau (eds) *Theoretical models and processes of reading* (5th edn) (pp. 1570–1613). Newark: DE: International Reading Association.

Linn, S. (2004). *Consuming kids: Protecting our children from the onslaught of marketing and advertising.* New York: Anchor.

Luke, A., & Freebody, P. (1999). Further notes on the four resources model. *Reading online.* Retrieved from http://www.readingonline.org/research/lukefreebody.html

McCartney, S. (2007, May 15). Why those government stats on airlines are misleading. *Wall Street Journal,* pp. D1, D4.

Moses, R.P. & Cobb, C.E., Jr. (2001). *Radical equations.* Boston, MA: Beacon Press.

Nagda, A.W. & Bickel, C. (2000). *Tiger math.* New York: Macmillan.

National Council of Teachers of English. (2004). NCTE beliefs about the teaching of writing. Retrieved from http://www.ncte.org/positions/statements/writingbeliefs

National Council of Teachers of English. (2008). The NCTE definition of 21st century literacies. Retrieved from http:www.ncte.org/positions/statements/21stcentdefinition

National Council of Teachers of Mathematics. (2000). *Principles and standards for school mathematics.* Reston, VA: National Council of Teachers of Mathematics.

New York Times (1989, December 24). Portrait of the 1980's: Selections from 10 years of history. *New York Times.* Retrieved from http://www.nytimes.com

Orrill, R. (1997). Foreword. In L.A. Steen (ed.) *Why numbers count: Quantitative literacy for tomorrow's America* (pp. xi–xiv). New York: College Entrance Exam Board.

Portalupi, J., & Fletcher, R. (2001). *Nonfiction craft lessons: teaching information writing k-8.* Portland, ME: Stenhouse.

Rabin, R. (2009, March 26). Proximity to fast food a factor in student obesity. *New York Times,* p. A16.

Rosenbaum, D. (2003, February 25). Washington memo: The President's tax cut and its unspoken numbers. *New York Times.* Retrieved from http://www.nytimes.com

Saul, S. (2008, October 8). Experts conclude Pfizer manipulated studies. *New York Times,* p. B4.

Schuman, H., & Scott, J. (1987). Problems in the use of survey questions to measure public opinion. *Science,* 236(4804), 957–959.

Schwartz, S., & Whitin, D.J. (2006). Graphing with four-year olds: Exploring the possibilities through staff development. In P. Elliott (ed.) *Teaching and learning mathematics* (NCTM Yearbook), (pp. 5–16). Reston, VA: National Council of Teachers of Mathematics.

Spirer, H.F., Spirer, L., & Jaffe, A.J. (1998). *Misused statistics.* New York: Marcel Dekker.

Steen, L.A. (1997a). Preface: The new literacy. In L.A. Steen (ed.) *Why numbers count: Quantitative literacy for tomorrow's America* (pp. xv–xxviii). New York: College Entrance Examination Board.

Steen, L.A. (ed.) (1997b). *Why numbers count: Quantitative literacy for tomorrow's America.* New York: College Entrance Examination Board.

Steen, L.A. (1999). Numeracy: The new literacy for a data-drenched society. *Educational Leadership,* 57(2), 8–13.

Steen, L.A. (2001a). Mathematics and numeracy: Two literacies, one language. *The Mathematics Educator*, 6(1), 10–14.

Steen, L.A. (ed) (2001b). *Mathematics and democracy*. Washington, DC: National Council on Education and the Disciplines.

Steen, L.A. (January 2007a). Every teacher is a teacher of mathematics. *Principal Leadership*, 7(5), 16–20.

Steen, L.A. (November 2007b). How mathematics counts. *Educational Leadership*, 65(3), 9–14.

Swarns, R. (2008, September 16). Capitol strives to define "homeless." *New York Times*, p. A15.

Tierney, J. (2009, June 30). Calculating consumer happiness at any price. *New York Times*, p. D.1, D.6.

Tufte, E.R. (1983). *The visual display of quantitative information*. Cheshire, CT: Graphics Press.

Tukey, J. (1997). *Exploratory data analysis*. Boston, MA: Addison-Wesley.

Vasquez, V. (2004). *Negotiating critical literacies with young children*. Mahwah, NJ: Erlbaum.

Vasquez, V. (2010). *Getting beyond "I like the book." Creating space for critical literacy in k-6 classrooms* (2nd edn). Newark, DE: International Reading Association.

Whitin, B., & Dobur, J. (2009). An analysis of past significant inflow events into Lake Sidney Lanier. *Proceedings of the 2009 Georgia Water Resources Conference* held April 27–29 at the University of Georgia. Retrieved from http://www.srh.noaa.gov/alr/papers/content/lanier.pdf

Whitin, D.J. (1997). Collecting data with young children. *Young Children*, 52(2), 28–32.

Whitin, D.J. (2006). Learning to talk back to a statistic. In P. Elliott (ed.) *Teaching and learning mathematics* (NCTM 2006 Yearbook) (pp. 31–40). Reston, VA: National Council of Teachers of Mathematics.

Whitin, D.J., & Whitin, P. (1998). Learning is born of doubting; Cultivating a skeptical stance. *Language Arts*, 76(2), 123–129.

Whitin, D.J., & Whitin, P. (1999). Mathematics is for the birds: Reasoning for a reason. In L. Stiff (ed.) *Developing mathematical reasoning, K-12*. (NCTM 1999 Yearbook) (pp. 107–114). Reston, VA: National Council of Teachers of Mathematics.

Whitin, D.J., & Whitin, P. (2003). Talk counts: Discussing graphs with young children. *Teaching Children Mathematics*, 10(3), 142–149.

Whitin, D.J., Mills, H., & O'Keefe, T. (1990). *Living and learning mathematics*. Portsmouth, NH: Heinemann.

Whitin, P., & Whitin, D.J. (1997). *Inquiry at the window*. Portsmouth, NH: Heinemann.

Whitin, P., & Whitin, D.J. (2003). Developing mathematical understanding along the yellow brick road. *Young Children*, 58(1), 36–40.

Whitin, P., & Whitin, D.J. (2008). Learning to read the numbers: A critical orientation toward statistics. *Language Arts*, 85(6), 432–441.

Wilhelm, J. (2006). The age for drama. *Educational Leadership*, 63(7), 74–77.

Williams, J., & Joseph, G. (1993). Statistics and inequality: A global perspective. In D. Nelson, G. Joseph, & J. Williams (eds) *Multicultural mathematics: Teaching mathematics from a global perspective* (pp. 175–204). Oxford: Oxford University Press.

Winerip, M. (2006, May 17). Odd math for "Best High Schools" list. *New York Times*, p. B.9.

Wood, G. (2004). A view from the field: NCLB's effects on classrooms and schools. In D. Meier, A. Kohn, L. Darling-Hammond, T. Sizer, & G. Wood (eds) *Many children left behind* (pp. 33–52). Boston, MA: Beacon Press.

Index